MY COUNTRY

Collected Poems

My Country

ALISTAIR ELLIOT

Collected Poems

CARCANET

First published in 1989 by
CARCANET PRESS LIMITED
208-212 Corn Exchange
Manchester M4 3BQ

British Library Cataloguing in Publication Data
Elliot, Alistair, *1932-*
Collected Poems.
I. Title
821' .914

ISBN 0-85635-846-0

The Publishers acknowledges the financial assistance of
the Arts Council of Great Britain.

Typeset by Bryan Williamson, Manchester
Printed in England by SRP Ltd, Exeter

CONTENTS

I New Poems – "The American Poems"

II Other uncollected new poems

I

New Poems
"The American Poems"

My country, 'tis of thee,
Sweet land of liberty,
    Of thee I sing:
Land where my fathers died,
Land of the pilgrims' pride,
From every mountain-side
    Let freedom ring.

Words: "America" (Samuel Francis Smith, (1808-1895)
Tune: Composer unknown; used as the British national anthem from c.1745

America: a Love Poem

Once I could swim across to kiss you; then
I'd have to yoke my giant dragonflies
To the canoe you left behind – remember
You wove me a sail of palm-fronds to blow home with?
Then the green sunset of your hair
Behind an arc of sea – you seemed to sleep
Further and further round the room, too far
To hear whether you answered my Good-night.

Your creatures changed their looks. I know because
Sometimes embarrassed birds arrived,
Unrecognised, and couldn't see a mate
In the small brown females of our flying snakes.
Sometimes an edible root or fruit was brought,
Surprising me: new forms and dangerous colours,
And tastes of frogspawn or the spit of bees.
Could you be different, smiling face of earth?

My creatures may have quietly changed, and I,
Massaged by icy irresponsible hands,
Have lost my youthful wrinkles and that sharp
Crystalline look you loved to lie to west of
At dawn. But you'll be beautiful always. Always
I long for you. Drift back again, and roll
Under my sandy shoulders, O escaped
Land of my childhood, O America!

Emigrants from Sutherland

May 1848

"What with their songs, their music, and the beating of their feet, as they danced under the inspiration both of whisky and pipes, there was a tolerable noise kept up till daylight. But... it was impossible and unjust to be angry with the poor fellows..." Charles St. John, 1849

We steam past Handa Island: the birds stay
Forever, laying eggs for someone else,
And when we've all left, laying for themselves.

Is this like dying? I feel sick and free,
Lifted so easily towards the sky.

Inland, the gentleman with the boat on wheels
Has set off osprey-fishing in the hills,
So gently preying on the birds of prey...

I shall be free as him when we step out
In Arcady, where the ospreys nest in trees
And the people live in wood instead of stone,
Where no one has to send away for grain
Or leave his land to work, and no one dances
The exiles' dance, *America*, all night...

At Sea

for Amanda

Lying beside you, shadowed by the jenny
All morning, genially talking in the rubber
Boat on the foredeck – it's how the landlubber
Imagines sailing: cream, in a great vee
Unzipping, which we draw across the sea,
And blue, broken by dolphins for a while
And (fluttering at the bosom of a sail)
Perhaps a lost emigrant butterfly.

Our lifeboat sags, and we bump pleasantly.
In five nights I'll be reckoning at the wheel
The heights of seas – could we untie that boat
Before we sink? – how long could swimmers float
Among these soft ravines? – can this be real? –
Trapped among particles of reality.

Wetting Yourself

(Thanksgiving Day 1983)

At a strange distance from my dictionary
I ponder "bilge" – a fine word to be found
Wearing about your head the night you're drowned –
And steer, looking the zephyr in the eye.

The main flaps, ghost of an expensive sail.

The engine-head's cracked. You scoop diesel stink
From under floorboards straight down *Emilie's* sink –
Jack still works, when the pumps and radio fail.

The sea's worse, but my stomach's now quite calm:
I spell you bailing.
                                        The sink blocks.
                                                                        We pour
The bilge on the self-draining cockpit floor.

Drenched with the Gulf Stream spray (too warm for harm?)
In the cold wind I ponder "piss myself",
Forty miles out on the continental shelf.

Another Day

Wedged in behind the table, on the floor
In a damp blanket: it's Jack's turn to steer,
My turn to sleep. Just under my left ear
The keel thumps water – or the Florida shore?
The mast tries to unstep itself – I'm curled
Beside its stormy knowledge like a snake.

The moon's framed in a hatch when I awake:
God! I'm in outer space, and that's the world...

Jack's calling: he's seen dolphins in the air,
Rolling down mountain-waves. Still wet, I climb
The oily steps into another time:
The hemisphere's so bright! And the wind fair...

High on the bucking boat, I laugh at the sun,
My equal: "Sol! Dear Jewish relative,
So glad to see you" – and as glad to live
As if I were fifteen, not fifty-one.

For now the greater light of Genesis
Leans through the firmament with a long, dry kiss.

Making Land

Coming to port at night, you only see
Abstractions: something fixed, a wooden solid
Where large cleats perch, an elephantine bollard
And barnacles nailed at the level of your eye.

Flicked by a greyish handkerchief of light,
You wake at a latitude and longitude
Here too, but at the alarm-call of a bird...

Its screams are colourful, all but literate –
The diva of an opera for parrots.

On deck you finally see the ominous, tropical
Shape of this bird, parrot in mourning: grackle,
Which cries pollution: rigging! bilge! ships' cats!
– And noise!
For here walks roaring round the dock
A dustman with a vacuum on his back.

Discovery

Snow covers all the summer history
Of this place: only the wooden people
With shrugging arms, the feathery
Dancers, completely non-political,
Seem to have lived here, ever.
They stand, deferring slowly to each other,
Up to their knees in granulated water,
Obviously unfit to represent
The obliterated voters of a planet,

But there is no-one else: that snow
Came in and silenced the discussion.
Now the arboreal view
Is all that's left of evolution.
What happened here? I wander
Into the culture of the conifer
To find some facts, a rather mobile stranger
Apparently come to judge the very slow.
But these are trees of ignorance: they are frozen.

I'm walking through an accident
Of the universe which would be pretty
If the sun shone on it –
In the cold estimate of my eye.
This world is not so good
In a poor light. To think a passing cloud
Can put that innocent radiation out!
Killing precipitates of heaven . . . I crush
The six-armed crystals into plaques of slush.

Now here's a shelter, on a knoll
Above a stream: it's made of cylinders
Arranged at a rational angle,
Biting each other at the corners.
Some enemy to reason,
Offended by the straightness of a line,
Has broken it. The geometry's caved in.
And there's a mound, about my length; it looks
Like a person, hibernating in a bag –

I think, the creature that made the cabin.
I can not touch it. With a stick
I rummage for its open
Snow-choked mouth. It tears and leaks
Dark matter, leaves, and rot.
The unexamined object like a threat
Gapes at me, crammed with questionable meat
Like a full snake. What horror have I found?
My duty says, Look into it. But I can't.

I stumble away; I pass the night
Wrestling with Sleep, the brother of Death,
Beside the little gate
Of absence somewhere in the head;
I know I must go back.
And when I do, bending beside my tracks
And freeing the bag from white stuff with one tug,
I find it's empty. All it had contained,
The evil of a world, was in my mind.

Dinosaur Stop in Arizona

Maybe there's something wrong with us. The rest
of our inquisitive species is at home
staring into the windows of nowhereland
or doing homework or at least
turning a fellow-creature into food.

Even the owners of these souvenir-shacks
have slid off their stools into the dusk
for a little happy-hour sex
on the creaking desert sand
before the stars emerge and look.

But we, most curious of all, have come
to pry into the earth's ill-kept diaries.
At the page open here
a creature with three fat toes upon a foot
as big as an adult human hand

walked through a patch of mud.
Not a moment worth recording for the beast,
a perfect entry for today: we stand
and listen by the stone-cold track.
It walked away among unpetrified trees.

Two Cats in New Hampshire

for Don and Jane

The perforated barn tries to keep out
This summer like the older hotter summers,
But samples of today's light,
Already dusty, lean in corners.
A careful husband would collect
Spiderwebs here for his new wife's new dress,
Dearer than silk; the kittens came and picked
A bat for breakfast, full of insect juice,
Or sun-demented flies.
It was built to hold treasure, and it does.

The house was built, not by one grandfather
But others, earlier, room by room,
Cells for the honey of him and her,
The unconsumable taste of home.
I itch, slightly, to be off,
As if seeing the footprints of a bear
In the deep woods were what I must achieve:
As if I could not just sit pickling here.
The cats can, staying indoors forever
Now the road's busier. They have each other.

Being a lovable cat is good:
Regular features, regular meals.
But don't they long for chickadee blood?
To clean their teeth with chipmunk tails?
They had their curiosities cut off,
Of course. Could I be calm like them
Without my sausage and its bag of stuff?
Those seeds, like marjoram, a dust of thyme,

Season our wholesome but monotonous moods.
Without them, we'd have just the thing that broods.

The thing that broods, impatient in the head,
Fingers the fate of these two animals
Preserved like harvest in a box: I brood
Upon the variety of pleasant jails,
Where it does not appear the air's been censored,
The messages of water scrambled: I brood
Most on my prayer for nomadism, answered
With this disease of travelling from food
To food that other creatures gather,
As if the goddess of fortune were my mother.

Inside, my friend prays to his dictaphone.
Outside, the singing silence, tinnitus
Of crickets, leads me on.
The flies are out of season, but saws buzz
Angrily in some transept of the woods.
Over the still green leaves some bird of prey
Cries a fair warning as I find the treads
The bear left for me. Should I stay
To dance among the boles with him? Or home
On my old friends, open the caddy and brew up for them?

What is my treasure, bears or the tea-brewing
With cats in their old wooden kitchen?
On my way back, I see a beaver drawing
Right across Eagle Pond his thoughtful line,
Like the path of the scissors cutting up
A western territory,
Trampling the water almost in his sleep:
Calm owner of the pond and its periphery,
However large, calm cutter of the trees,
Unable to see that they are someone else's.

A Corner Room at the Ansonia

It's dawn in the Americas. I peer
Out of my blanket at the tops of trees:
No wind; and the crossed fingers of teepees
Against the light swear that today is clear.

Why have I slept outdoors? That parallel
Herringbone sky looks wrong. Why is it square?
The Great Plains should be perfuming the air,
But I taste nothing...
                                        It's my city cell:
Pot-plants, an easel, looking Indian.

What woke me isn't that I sense the whites
Are massing, but some lack of oxygen –
A need not thought of in the Bill of Rights.

The window's jammed shut. On my heels I sit
Beside the run of dreams. This wilderness
Bears food and drink. If you've the craft for it,
You can live well, ignoble savages.

A New York Accountant

A simple self in trousers and a shirt
sits barefoot at my desk: beside this rock
sheltering in the wilderness of New York.
He's eating some primeval food, the sort
you swallow on stage, a chaos of white dirt
such as an archaeologist who can cook
uncovers in a megalithic stomach –
"Rice pudding," he says, offering to share it.

He found it down the canyon, down the street;
he gets in with a key to do the accounts,
works when it suits him, free-lance, at odd moments,
and is the brother of a famous poet.

Grinning, he seems to sit there in disguise,
a hunter-gatherer from another tribe,
with a pale, fresh look, as if I'd made him wipe
a beautiful layer of warpaint off his face.

Near the Frick Collection

It must be nice to live on Central Park...

This man lives in it. Marvellous address;
No mail though, and no residence till dark.
He's clearing out his place now, in distress
Swinging from bag to bag like an old lion,
Behind the little bars of rain. Could be
He just collects those magazines to lie on,
Could be the archive of his poetry,
A life's work anyway: his papers, wet
And turning to mâché, and still unread
Because he has no street-lamp by his bed.
He makes no answer to my how-do-you-do? –
Why should he? It's his room I'm tracking through,
As I go muddily towards the Met.

Our Country

A letter of condolence

My dear, You can imagine from what people
I hide to write, pretending natural need,
Which I can say it is, to write to you
About our loss. For George was mine as well,
Though I could not admit him to my table.
You gave him his sweet nature, but he was
Always my boy, my self, my other eyes,
My second body, as much as he was yours.
Fathers do grieve, you know: we may look hard,
Separate in our lives and uniforms,

Unable to display our love in public;
But as you know from many happy hours,
We are as soft and sensible as women,
And as this paper shows, we too can weep.

At this important time, when what I do
May help to make our many states unite
As one, I cannot come to you and speak
As I would wish, the halting words of comfort.
I know that it's the voice and hand that comfort
And not the word, and I must hope that you
Will blame the time, the run of destiny
That carries me away, and not blame me
For being distant now. It's not my pride,
My vanity in being white, as you
May think, that stops me coming, but my work,
Our country's work. It would be just the same
If George had been a son I could acknowledge
And follow into church and stand above
And throw the earth upon. My dear, dear friend,
Forgive this terrible absence, which is terrible
For both of us. Meanwhile, I'm sure your mistress
Has been as kind as I could be. You know
She's a good woman: she can understand.
George in a way was hers, as she's my wife.

Still, I address this letter, our first letter,
In care of Julius. I hope that you can read it –
I've written it as steadily as I can.
Now I must go. I am, as they say here,
As ever, your obedient humble servant,

T.

Networks

End of the party: time to offer friends
To the foreigner.
                    – Where are you going, sir?
– North for a bit, then west.
                                        Ed recommends
An Apache sculptor, aura-balancer,
Wells Fargo money-minder to the stars,
Ethnomusician. Tom and Marion
Give me an acupuncturist near Taos,
A Persian-carpet-dealer in Tucson,
A Choctaw woman (pity, no address),
A graphics programmer with a private press...

Such generous social helpings! In a year
I shall have friends to offer these friends to:
Expert on hunger, film-sound-engineer,
Inventor of the Pill, a southern Jew,
A goy psychiatrist, gay classicist,
Redneck philosopher, holist, black girl deck-hand,
Wigmaker, pulmonary therapist,
Yoga carpenter, Chinese diamond-merchant,
Hard-riding, yachting septuagenarians...

At home, I just know poets and librarians.

Three Cats in California

These cats watch me – here comes company –
As I emerge
Dragging a cushion, sniffing an orange,
Onto my wooden balcony.
To them I'm more remarkable
Than the sun hobbling up over the ridge is,
Grasping redwoods like spears or crutches,
Till suddenly as good as new
It vaults into the air – and does not fall.

The salted world's still sweating dew.
A bobcat slopes off through the loaded grasses.
The huge green wafer steams with morning scent.
Nothing distracts these three from what they want:
Pure attention, and maybe some caresses.
Has word got round that I can speak
Their language? But I growl:
Right now I can't be affable.
Yes, nothing has been going on for hours,
But what I sit here doing is work:
Opening the orange and the mind, in hemispheres.

Waved off, the tabby cat, the grey, the red
(With a great scar across its back)
Scrabble along a ledge to the sun-deck.
So they're excluded,
Today, again. But they can wait,
Imagining their entrance in the end
To our nests of luxury, their word of command
To the obedient fridge.
They see coming what I do not:
Their golden age.

Disconsolate now, they do have friends – or could
Be making friends, I think: a skunk,
In a whirlpool of its sleepy stink,
Was dancing nervously on the brow of the road
Yesterday, and I've seen them leave a meal
For the raccoons at midnight: delicate
Maskers tripping forward to the plate,
Bowing, a courteous peck, and back,
Into the shade. But these are only cordial
With food: they do not speak: they aren't romantic.
There is such friendship in a human being!
The cats promise themselves one each . . .

Meanwhile, flat out, they watch,
Dangling their hairy arms from branches; doing
Their work invisibly as mine; without a squeak
Clearing the area of mice.
Mice have been seen inside the house,
But still these cats must stay outdoors: their fur

Carries the burning oil of poison oak.
They are untouchable. They must live out there.

They see I've analysed my orange.
Alma is sitting in her dressing-gown
In the meadow, writing; John
Steps thoughtfully towards the kitchen range.
Others under our common roof
Still have their noses in a dream.

All day one separates oneself from them.
A spirit who would like to join
Must whisper in the wood, aloof,
Till sunset; then, rubbing the window pane,
May watch us share the fire, the food, the wine.

The Melting Pot

Now we become a crew.
                                        The skipper steers
In through the islands, dark and getting darker,
And we all scan the night for the first marker.
Two have sailed here before, but not for years.

Our light winks, twice. Campfires of savages
Flicker through trees. Keep sounding: it's low tide:
The shafts of grasses nearly reach our side.

"No wash," a signpost in the water says.
We drop sails with a sigh.
                                        The chart rubs past
Under our fingers, light by light. We feel
In the perineum
             mud
                wiping the keel
And in the skull
             a bridge
                     cropping the mast.

At Harbour Town, no longer tall and deep
And multiple, we separate and sleep.

Susanna Undressing

The apartment's full of pictures of you – odd
Consequence of your exile – none as good
However, as the Rembrandt in my head.

This is the one you'd want. My retina,
Passing along the corridor, flicked: you cower
In the impenetrable atmosphere

Of a bedroom, golden in the corner light;
Shadows and angles, arms holding up weight,
A shirt perhaps, make shelter for the fruit

That hangs with shocking roundness. In a gallery
I'd have turned back to watch the slightly furry
Globes still floating. In the light of memory

I hold the single frame and wonder if
This was a view you wanted to engrave
Somewhere, and I was all you seemed to have.

Visiting the Astrologer

I

Lindsay was driving, with her favourite
Passenger, smiling naturally, on her right,
So I got in behind, my nose and chin
Wagging and sniffing at the strangers' skin,
The presences of amiable women.

As we swung up and down the grid impressed
On San Francisco's many-breasted chest,
Ellie was saying, "Why don't we stop off
At the Soviet Embassy to inscribe our love
And sympathy for losing Andropov?"

Why should she want to make the Soviet scene?
She saw a programme on the household screen
About the suffering of American comrades...
Or does she think that she's descended from a
Victorian Russian trapping in Sonoma?

I was about to say I hate to sign
Subscription lists; but first, "There'd be a line,"
Said Lindsay, "and we haven't time to wait."
For we were driving north a hundred eighty
Miles to consult the reader of their fate.

After Mount Tam, the hosts and guest agree
The winter light just kills the scenery
Of U S 101: it's a dull day, and
Even the good old car starts to complain.
When we turn off, it stops, and says it's dying.

It feels as if we've left America:
The playful journey, pure control and power,
Ends in the streaming silence of a lane
Among wet pines, and Lindsay in the rain
Taking the engine's pulse with slow disdain.

Ellie's the prettiest: she walks off to tease
Some local help from somewhere in the trees.
It's an adventure! Someone stops it, though,
By joining wires – and Lindsay has to go
And rescue Ellie from some smiling fellow.

II

Petronia welcomes us as if she knew
We would be late; her baby's also due...
All hug each other. I'm the only man –
Wise women don't need husbands for conception –
They buy good sperm, a tube of Californian.

We crowd the wooden room: its furniture,
Shrouded and heaped for painting, is the future,
Leaning towards us in a bulging membrane
I try to ignore; they've come to see it plain,
To make the thing that's going to happen happen.

It seems that Fate allows a choice – this nice
Near-mother tells them how, and gives advice.
I don't see Lindsay paying for prophecies:
She's been a lawyer: she knows how money flies.
The sweetness of credulity must be Ellie's;

Who has begun to charm me, now she shows
More than one ear, one cheek, and half a nose.
Over a dusty coffee we decide
I shall go find the Pacific where it hides
Quietly in mist; they'll stay and mistily confide.

The land stops, torn away casually.
I try to imagine Petronia's surgery,
Where a bland faith is calming the high hand
Of reason: Lindsay wants to buy an island,
But "Will my friend come with me to my land?"

Love is confusion. But the lovable
Ellie has learned to keep her questions simple.
They like to sit and write in bed; they've just
Finished a script: what should they start on next? –
She names the customers and the range of subjects.

While she entrusts their destiny to a star,
An oily man haruspicates the car.
It needs some work which can't be done on Sunday.
So Lindsay's bought three toothbrushes. We must stay,
At the Sea Gull Inn, in "The Barn". Three beds. No hay.

III

A pleasant murmur and giggling of friends
In the shower, a hissing silence when it ends –
I lie and look at the wall. The paper shows
Pawmarks of bears – they seem to jog in rows –
Or holy writ, the growl of Hebrew prose.

We seem to be escaping off the scale
Of the predictable, two females and a male
Circling for holds, till pleasure finds its level.
But Ellie rings her home, and, "Patrick's ill,"
She tells us – and abruptly goes maternal.

The fever far away enfeebles us.
All we can think of is the morning bus.
The waiter's well-learned hymn to the cuisine
Stirs nothing, all enjoyment's now indecent
And even early bed's a bit obscene.

There I sink inward, through the sounds of the sea
And amorous frogs that drown the breaths of Ellie
Alone in her double bed across the floor.
At dawn she quietly slips from the adventure
Like Captain Oates whispering au revoir.

IV

And at breakfast, suavely mouthing my French toast
As great waves chew the Mendocino coast,
I find I too am looking back: Today
Is the first of ever after, a speechless Monday
When people have to work, cars don't, and Lindsay

Is doomed to wait, but wishes I would go.
She tells me (walking off) to call the radio,
And raise my voice and offer "British poet
Wanting a lift" to the atmospheric market –
Which might make Chapter One of my next hit.

How does a man decide what next? To go
For redwoods, Russian River, Silverado?
Falling alone in social space, I'm free
But long for some co-ordinates, some gravity.
What would Petronia have to say to me?

I can't go there! She thinks the universe
Has plans, and shares them with astrologers!
I dip in Chance's river, State Route One,
And soon I'm travelling south with a brave woman
Who lives by making up a Magic Lotion.

Sometimes she needs to escape her ideal life
In the commune. I guess she's someone's wife...
I buy some cream (for Lindsay's hot-tub skin)
In thanks. Then I drift home. I think I've chosen:
I want to visit Ellie's voice again.

A Case of Identities

Needlepoint Park: in the Utopia
I've just begun my bacon and home-fries
And eggs, I'm squinting at my newspaper,
When this black man starts giving with the eyes.
He's more than friendly, in this rugger shirt,
And calls, "It's *Different Strokes*, right?" Like a dope,
Slowly, I see he isn't trying to flirt –
He thinks I'm someone in a TV soap.
Too bad I'm not. And maybe I should do
His number and be Mr Drummond, once...
But then I notice he's like someone too:
The oval face of a Nigerian bronze.
  I stare and stare. But it would not be cool
  To tell this stranger, now, he's beautiful.

The Writer's Place

She was quite small; there's her bed,
a place for curling up and shrinking, not
for soldering cells or getting bigger in.

Here at this window she made the lonely words
notice each other's arms: they would unite
like dogs, never to part again,

as her big brother, on the floor below
or leaning fully dressed on the piano,
lifted his terrifying probe

into the universe of her editor –
whose skirts flew upward neatly from the waist
and never got creased, but covered her top completely.

Two frilly stalks held up this flower with, flaring
between, her "odorous nebula": she was married
to a quite small astronomer called David...

It's possible our small heroine could hear
these explorations from her narrow stair,
but this is all we know:

pieces for four legs and piano
were never added to her repertoire.

Their intertwining names no longer grow
over the house. It's her place now.

A Solipsist in the South

You think, so I exist:
You are a Thinking Being,
And I am one of the Thoughts.

"But Hunt, how can I be
A Thought? I'm an Old Friend!"

You were strangely nice to a Thought,
That sunny November day:
You drove me to Harper's Ferry,
Explained the Civil War –
Uh, War between the States.

True, I was nice, yesterday,
When you asked to be left alone
In our room with a feminine Thought.

Today though, I resist:
"How d'you account for a Thought
That says you're thinking crap?"

"I'm dreaming that part of me
Disagrees with another part.
You understand – the cosmos
Is not my wish-fulfilment:
It's a game I seem to be playing
With all the sides of myself."

"But the world is independent
Of us: there are other wills,
And rules; it continues to change
Whether we watch or not.
It obeys the laws of physics,
Not the whims of a brain.
Doesn't it shake your theory
When the news is not your style –
Too funny or foul, or about
Places you never heard of ,
In somebody else's language?"

"What d'you think my subconscious
Is doing now, while I talk?
Why, it's developing history
Everywhere . . . "

I didn't ask
How you explained your divorce,
Your having to stay by the phone
Because you were selling your car,
Your friends with rooms and arms.
I thankfully ate the chop
You fried me for early breakfast –
Hot breakfast for a Thought! –
And hugged you, and caught my bus
Out of your mind to my old
School in the Blue Ridge Mountains;
To sea, and a storm that tried
To wash you out of my notebook;
To three-piece suites on porches,
And enormous automobiles;
To spinach salad, eaten
On a British Battlefield;
To the half-remembered world
Of unthinkable America,
Where I see a sign from a window:

"You have arrived in the best
Place you could possibly be,
Spartanburg South Carolina,
And we're glad you're here."

The Question of Food

Sunday October 26, 1986

How do these things become us? – orange juice
as we cast off, fudge as we meet the ocean
funnelling into the inlet of Cape May, then
boiled chestnuts, grey and wrinkled as the seas
our stomachs ride (the heaving field of Delaware Bay)
all morning, and for lunch a chocolate kiss
and an apple from the pollen of two trees
sensibly rooted, restaurants of bees . . .

What can our helpless tissues make of this?

Coasting on glacier mints and peppermint tea
like an experiment, we come to Ocean City,
lassoo some posts for *Emilie* to nuzzle
in the dark, after her evening drink of diesel,
and sink into the cabin where already
there's crabmeat fried in butter, and sashimi
(tuna as soft as jelly), steak, and salad.

Somehow the four tall engines are refuelled
by this: we smile, and share the mystery.

In the Marina at Hilton Head Island

Are boats named in the office (*Ocean Beauty*,
Vagabond, *Tyche*), lying by the hearth
(*Boss Lady*), or in someone else's bath
(*Stitchwitch*, *The Nauti-Lady*, *The Big Cutie*)?

It seems men name them, hardly thinking (*Press
On Regardless!*), jokes hovering above the cheque
(*On Business*, *Ramblin' Wreck* of Georgia Tech),
And own them guiltily (*African Princess*).

Women seem absent, laughing (*Miss Me II,*
Sea Tabby IV), so *Happy Pelican*
Admits, like others, he's no sailorman –
Just a shy little camper in the blue.

Have women too much sense to join this team?
(All I can find is *Idyll Ours* to show
Anyone hoped for company.) They know
The dream of boats: wet, lonely, masculine dream.

The working boats are different: at the pier
A fisherman sold us for twelve dollars all
The shrimps he'd caught that evening in his trawl;
His wife was there; the boat was called *Maria*.

In Memory of November 29th, 1983

for Jack Brod

Down Mosquito Lagoon, rain-shadows fall
Powdering the bonsai islands – MANATEE
CAUTION (Are mermaids of this Inland Sea
So dangerous?) – Again we use up all
Transmission fluid, near Canaveral –
I lose my cap, getting the jib-sheet free –
Mermaids, you wear it, and imagine me –
By dusk, the Apollo gantries look quite small.
At Dragon Point we turn for
                    Damn, the boat
Hits a reef in the channel, thirty feet
Clear of the marker –
                U.S. Engineers,
We curse you! Words unfit for soldiers' ears! –

We're stuck: Scotch on the rocks seems fitting – Neat?
Jack's birthday party (74)'s afloat...

Swimming in Florida Again

Swimming down with a breadknife through the gloom,
Shy in my briefs, I hack the rope wrapped round
The prop. Four dives. It streaks without a sound
Of parting from this dusty, airless room.

The prop-blades cut my knuckles. In these waters
The Atlantic carries salt for wounds. I shiver,
Still hacking: are there sharks in Indian River,
Reef-haunting mothers with a million daughters?

I daren't look – depths scare me – but haul my legs
Into the rubber lifeboat (watch the knife!) –
Tired of the sea, not of terrestrial life.

Up there, a concrete dragon on the hill
Lours in the rain over its steaming eggs.

I feel the imagined teeth upon me still.

Reasons for Happiness in San Francisco

for Marion Maitlis

I

Breakfast can always be the same.
The mind in the morning likes to hover
Over its habits: food as happiness,
Opening an orange as a form of power.

II

If I have two brains in my head,
Today their marriage is happy:
One lets the other learn to draw –
While thinking to itself the caption
"Learning to draw in California!"

III

The phone-calls are not all for Stanley,
Coiffeur of wigs, painter of bodies –
This one's for me. She says
She's printing. Am I strong?
Maybe I'll help her with the presswork? Sure!
A smile into the mouthpiece for next month.

IV

There are pleasures in maintenance:
Buying stationery (on Haight);
Leaving my Harris wool
Sportsjacket to be cleaned, by a Chinese,
Of its American dust;
Sending some books to the future sadder me;
Writing "Forgive me" to an injured friend.

V

There's also conquest, my new territory
Called Golden Gate Park.
I'm proud of the Mesozoic patch:
The tree-ferns, the squawking jay
Like a model archaeopteryx,
The pool of green duck-soup (with ducks).
Of course, there are marauders in the bushes.
I let them have it, with both eyes.

VI

Food in art galleries
Is more fun.
Here you take lunch to a baroque
Fountain full of Zen
Boulders. I frighten a lady,
Being the happiest thing-in-clothes for miles.
This is what comes of reading Sarah Jewett
And eating ratatouille: rumination,
The dish of herbs that makes me think of you.

VII

Pictures, visible hours
Hung in this bank of time:
Some I don't like; but here I sip; and here
Is "Orpheus in Hades" by a friend of Bosch,
With a schoolgirl noting it – thin, pale brown,
And sad as an early Picasso.
No, older, an underpainted Botticelli.
Can her Andean shirt be warm?
She studies: my dead languages.
I wish her luck, meaning goodbye.

VIII

The heart, led beating away,
Is cool to Etruscan gems,
Tanagra bronze, Cycladic dolls,
Coins: the beautiful industry of art!
The heart is falling down its shaft.
"I want to see a person seeing."
The British portraits are all frowning.
Both of my brains are numb: "The Age of Rembrandt!"
But she comes back; she finds me: "Please,
What is the best Greek grammar-book?"
– Something to smile about.

IX

We walk among my rhododendrons, talking
A foreign code I learned at school,
Really just splashing in the bath
Of noman's language, friends.
Damn those marauders in the bushes:
She'll think I'm one of them.
We drink some tea at the museum, nomads
Pledging sweet home in camomile,
Under the waterfall of time.
Her friends are coming with a car. Friends?
Somehow she lends me ("au revoir")
A coin of happiness – a debt of honour.

X

The heart seems not to mind
Going backwards, alone, home;
Or that the mail's all junk today;
Or that I try again to draw.
It's reading something of its own
As I kiss Ramsay and Julie,
As I eat American cuisine,
As I walk back through Buena Vista Park.
It knows something is following,
The shy beast happiness,
To mark the steps of Stanley's house.

Meeting a Submarine

Seen by a creature on the water-skin
it was a lump; the horizon stung by a bee
was swelling; something barbed was stuck in the ocean.

A fishing-boat – no, a mound of boiling water
rushing us with a lance; I called the captain
out of the arms of Morpheus or whoever.

The sun was up. He was amused at me
still trembling as we met this tidal bore,
one of his nuclear subs going to sea.

The officers, mere bugs on a black tin can,
surveyed us grimly: if I photographed
their bow-wave they might turn and run us down.

They are going to the underworld for the winter.
No wonder they can't wave. In thought they've dived
already down the echoing corridor.

II

Other Uncollected New Poems

At Home with the Heavens

Few of us know the sky now. Pissing indoors,
How can you learn the dot-book of the stars?
Our unillumined country ancestors
Could read it over the shoulders of their lovers,
And in dark cities still be astronomers.

Ashamed perhaps, we skip the starry words
Of ancient poets – who end a storm "The clouds
Have run away, the Bears have reappeared,
And once again the vaporous Manger floats
Between the Donkeys" – images old and hard,

The lights of strangers. Now we use other signs
To pace our lives. And yet – most elements
Inside us are the dusty work of suns:
We should be recognising them as cousins,
Looking them up, reviving faint connections.

So once, at sea at midnight, told to steer
For a number on the card, I chose a star:
Caught in the diagram of shrouds, it flared,
A rage of light, with something softer, blurred,
Beside it. We were led across the seas
By both: Aldebaran and the Pleiades.

Twenty-Four Centuries Ago

for R.M. Ogilvie

"Lars Tolumnius" was otherwise engaged –
The messengers from Fidenae had to wait.
"Even the king of Veii has to crap,"
They thought at first, but after they had sat
Longer than even kings can spare for that,

They told the servant it was about the war
With Rome; so, grudgingly, he let them in.
Tulumnu, open fingers in mid-air
Over the war-game board, about to win,
Half-listened as they started to explain.

Rome had sent envoys: "They do not approve
Of our Etruscan pact. What shall we say?"
The king had thrown his dice; he made his move,
Saying "Kill" as we say "Mate" (the winning play),
Not noticing the messengers go away.

Bad luck for the four Romans, and for all
Who died as well in the ensuing wars,
Nobody seeing chance had made a pun.
"Large quantities of dice survive at Veii."
Made of the bones of those ambassadors?

The Sense of War

He ran, carrying you; it tilted down
Your street; it overtook you; the pale face
Of a gossip with a gun behind strange windows
Looked at you, and flew on to bomb the town.

I had been sent to safety, far away
(As you point out), to be brought up by women
To be less macho...
                                        Most days we went swimming
Inside our little reef. One winter day
Black smoke beyond the Gulf Stream sent distress
To the most neutral – even the fish below
In their transparency had felt the blow;
But we knew nothing, till across the surface
It reached
                    and touched us with its dirty hand.

My skin remembers war as oil and sand.

The Pranks of Totila

(552 A.D.)

It was well celebrated, his last day.
Totila made the delicate instrument
Of self resound, as great men learn to do
Always, as others do by accident.

Fresh with the virtue of not burning Rome
He rode out, as they looked at him, alone
Between the army from Byzantium
(Which we must call "the Romans") and his own

("The Goths"): a big man, dressed in golden armour,
On a gigantic charger, fluttering
With ribbons, like a legendary farmer
Winning the prizes in a country ring.

He showed them how a victor rides a horse,
Lying back as it caracoled and wheeled;
Spun in the saddle, juggling with spears
And pricking out the flowers of the field.

His enemies, John the Glutton and old Narses,
Watched till his vanity was satisfied –
Or till he turned away (his reinforcements
Had come at last). Later that day he died.

One of Our Submarines

We met a school, a family, or, we guessed,
a little university of dolphins,
that rolled around us, looking up with interest
at the full sails that pulled us by so fast,
with a sweet tickling, not the rub of engines.

I talked to them, but what have we to say
to the smiling scholars of the Scottish coast?
I was rude or boring. They took their children away
into the endless heaven of the sea,
leaving the polite benediction of the blest.

When I turned back to talk to you, I saw
an Ad Reinhardt black-on-black over your shoulder
whizzing sideways: it was a conning-tower,
with mariners waving: just a friendly power
of nature talking down to someone older.

To a Son in the Middle East

Now that I know you're safe, anxiety
Casts with another fly. Now that you write
"Verandah", with a "garden full of fruit",
I see a lizard humbly upside-down
Watching you read Herodotus; there's a fly
Slowly tacking towards the lizard's tongue.

And there's a charming rather sad young woman
Whose father is an officer who writes verse
In pencil on the back of battle-orders;
She hesitates by a fig-tree: is a fig
A proper gift to a foreigner in a room on
A hill? There's her timid, unfamiliar knock.

Is this the hill from which Tiglath-Pileser
Looked at the city on the eve of capture,
The kingdom Antony gave to Cleopatra
For a single kiss? If anything is given,
Make it the innocent kiss of sherbet: please her
With milk, snow, lemonade – as drunk in heaven.

Young women are always a bit imaginary;
But they're not treasure-trove. Their families
Still own them, watching there behind the trees
As the girl settles on your hand. Just try
To see her flight as they do: blow her free
Carefully as the angels flutter by.

Of course advice, the old man's voice, sounds shrill
To the young ear, and worse for being spelled
Out slowly. You would see the way I felt
Without such heavy words, if you were here:
Submissive to the inexperienced will
And interested in parental fear.

Taste Enhancers

An overdose of monosodium
Glutamate is like Sappho's medical
Account of love. Your blind spot starts to swell
And washes people in and out of the room
As you look round. An interesting game,
But you feel sick; and when you speak, you say,
"I'm eyes. I'm ternia's a float a way?"
You sweat. You shake. That small electric flame
Bobs about in your voice-box, out of reach –
So near the ammunition of the mind.
Is it a stroke? Too late you scribble, "Find
A blank tape" – to record your shuffled speech –
For now control comes back. Gears seem to meet
Again. A day in bed, and you recover.
You're sensitised for life, though, like a lover,
And there are things you can no longer eat.

The Quick

The little cut, right where I kiss, was deep.

But more than pain I felt the awkwardness
Of losing blood in public, the red mess
I make of secrets I'm too weak to keep.

I became one of those who bleed, unclean
And feared, the wounded dangerous inferior
Who bears nostalgic smells from the interior
Guiltily, half-recalling what they mean.

The ghost plays in its bath, while the blood drains.

The air, something invisible, came to kiss
And seal the pulsing in a cicatrice;
Something else calmed the excited little veins;
In all this there was nothing I could do...

All day I bled and was aware of you.

Recognition

On the Town Moor the butchers keep their cows,
A healthy hospice near the abattoirs.
Something is strange here, but they calmly browse,
Flicking flies with the nameplate in their ears,
And ruminate without conclusion, till
I cross the skyline.
                                        In my grey and blue
They recognise me on the man-made hill
And give a low, surprised, ancestral moo,
Wildly start up on high-heeled feminine feet,
And run to kiss me with a clumsy joy.
Their eyes, like goddesses', sadden when we meet:
I'm not their farmer, nor his bovine boy.

But still they stare, incredulous, in a trance:
Something has come again... A second chance...

Speaking of Larks

Suddenly larks are rare. A fertiliser kills
  The reasons for their song. Their landscape fills
  With whispers that some sharp-eared god enjoys,
  Papery music, low botanical noise.

Friends give each other names of fields not drugged, where birds
Still practise their ascensions on transparent words,
  Still disappear in light and silence where
  Nobody else can hide: a span of air.

You think of following them. The sound of summer now
Falls only from an aeroplane that echoes somehow
  In the soft sky. I'll find and interview
A lark with my machine...
                                        But will that comfort you?

Nature is leaving earth. The species one by one
Withdraw their voices. Soon the creatures shall have gone,
Leaving the subtle horns of rock for nitrogen
And oxygen and noble gas to play upon.

Burial Sentences

How wrong to come to Cambo
and not see you. But there it was, irrationally –
you were away. Even the piece of new
furniture in the chancel –
a thick and portable
six-sided table,
invisible apparently
to everyone but me –
had nothing to do with you.

The family faces gathered,
as long and thin and pale as yours, but brightening
to see each other. I wondered as we sang
if you could hear
wherever you were –
not in the varnished box,
perhaps outside with the far-seeing rooks
in the nest higher than the church –
the individual voices twining
such heavy strands of hymns, and recognise
the tones reluctant and deformed by sadness.

We sat to listen to the Book
of books, the comforter,
the old harmonious patchwork.
The Lord upholdeth all that fall,
and raiseth up all those that be bowed down
it would have said:
but we were given
the honest modern flour and water
and not the baked immortal bread
half-tasting of the Psalmist's oven.

How I would love to argue with you still
about the strength of words!
Your son read beautifully then,
calling you Pauline, as one soul
of another that has started heavenwards
to the simplicity from which we are fallen.

So did we all, I thought,
call you by that first name,
even perhaps the men and women
who saw you as a magistrate
and heard you utter the "fair sentences"
the preacher sought to praise:
beyond all titles still you were the same.

At last the voice of earth, the northern voice,
began: "Now lettest thou thy servant
depart in peace" –
and in the perfume of these ancient sounds

your light and folded garment,
shut in its wooden reliquary,
passed down the aisle, out of the breath of friends,
into the cold of January.

Under the sky Northumberland waits. Across
a field you knew by heart a young red horse
came galloping to see the earth receive
the measure of earth, the precious peck
of dust hidden away from sun and wind.
On the sharp drystone wall it leaned
its quizzical sorrel head, looking as you might look
on our casting crowns of flowers in your grave.

A Relic

Dazed by so many things to learn, alone
Among new heroes, none of them religious,
I forgot everything – except the bone,
The index finger that had christened Jesus.

Now I half wonder if I saw that thing I
Remember – it was thirty years ago –
And the label saying "John the Baptist's finger"
In brown ink, in a hurried hand, below.

It irritates the open mind – it lies
In me like an old bomb in a museum,
Live perhaps, as if waiting for its time,
Corroded skin containing a sweet juice,

A chrysalis of something I don't want.
And who does? That is not the way of faith
Nowadays, the hand of heaven underneath
The skirt of reason. So they've since withdrawn it –

The case holds something new now. But a bone
Was there... I hope they gave it to the dust
With honour. After all, it will have done
Some work, if not baptising him, for Christ.

Rooms

My favourite lavatory was on Ischia.
It was a small round tower on a flat roof,
Covered with plaster, vines and happy bees.
The humming might have been the sun, its rays
Shuffled in by the winking of a leaf
In the arrow-slit, or else mild snoring from a
Calmly-digesting-upside-down lucertola.
It was a shit-house nothing could improve.
It was my first Mediterranean summer.

If I could pick a bathroom too, I'd take
My friend Adrelia's one in Lower Hardacre
On the Lancastrian fells. Oh, it was large!
You lounged like Cleopatra in her barge,
The tub on a platform, space to swing a tiger
Under the low white eighteenth-century ceiling:
This was a place for the human body to mate
With the accommodating gods of water,
A place of skins and old religious feeling.

Have you the power, Muse, to add the kitchen
I love at Acomb? My friends are selling it,
And moving off the map to a Roman town,
Where they will cook ambrosia again
But not in a wooden box of words and heat,
With a milky-way of garlic in a bed
There, and a frame from Nature's exhibition
Here, uneasily looking in and out,
Like the soul ashamed of having to be fed.

Give me the bedroom with the cheap blue carpet
And home-made cupboards, where we watched the hares
Cavorting round their forms, and saw the fox
(Corrected by our little son to Vox)
Touring his fields, his land as much as ours.
We had to move, but carried off the room
In the box of memory like something sacred.
Allow us back to entertain our heirs –
I almost think you could untangle time.

That simple one-way tide makes such confusion.
How much we'd understand if we could stop it,
Wriggling between the forces and the spaces,
Through the transmission fluids of the species,
Beyond the black and white of the first planet.
There perhaps is the parlour of the dead,
Nothing like landscape, nebulous or Elysian,
Simply the dust, the gravitational carpet,
Toward which I walk with ever calmer tread.

A Highland View

Thanks to the glacier wearing down the gneiss,
The oldest rock of Britain, we have this view.
But somewhere under the smiling water
(No-one could mark the postcard with a cross)
Lay for a time, with Margaret Kerr, his wife,
Alistair Stewart, fisherman, of Nedd.

In the dark clothes of the maritime northern poor
I imagine them, my father's mother's parents,
Sinking unheard through salty darkening water,
Their boat drifting, their lobster-pots half lifted,
Their seven children ashore never to know
What happened, never to share a roof again.

The wool and serge and cotton might have come back,
Torn, unknown; but those who wore them last
Were mixed forever with other creatures
In the great bowl of Eddrachillis Bay
Far down in the reflective water,
Small variations in the youngest rock.

Sailing to Badcall

i.m. Alistair Elliot

It was a perfect day. They rigged the *Fern*
And set off down the loch before a wind
That blew from Eas Coul Aulin, three of them
Talking, my father in his fifteenth summer,
His father at the tiller, seventy-two,
And the second son, my uncle Alistair,
On his last holiday from the Glasgow bank,
Probably wishing that he'd brought his glasses.

They raced past Unapool, where William Daniel
Had sat drawing the lines of Ardaloch
Almost for them (Alistair had the engraving),
Looked back to Stack Glencoul and up Glendhu,
Gybed through the narrows at Kylesku where seals
Come to the ferry to improve their minds
And eat a fish, and still the wind and tide
Carried them out between the northern shore
And Calva where my father can remember
A reef with kelpy fingers reaching up
At *Fern's* white shadow, just a bit of gneiss
But turned to horror by a single fathom
Of clear Atlantic water.
                                        At the jetty
In Badcall Bay they got the year's provisions,
Left for them at the solitary warehouse
By MacBrayne's boat, and loaded up: four sacks
Of flour, two oats, one sugar and one salt,
A seven-pound tin of biscuits for his mother –
She liked rich-tea – perhaps a dram with Alec
The warehouse-man, a bite of bread and butter
Carried up high enough to sit and see
The Siamese island, Lewis-and-Harris, faint
And quiet beyond the roundness of the earth,
And waited for the moon to turn the tide.

The boat was heavy then; but with the breath
Of a westerly, they slid on the molten swell
Back beside Calva, past the broch to Kyle.
My father's father stopped at the hotel

And bought some water-of-life, for hospitality.
So they crept on, now rowing, all the way
Up the calm loch, cutting the mirror home.

As they came in, crossing the ring of islands,
The old man stood and tossed his folded jacket
Onto the shingle: a muffled sound of breakage,
A sense of thirsty cloth.
"And did he curse?"
"I never heard him say an angry word."

He would have thought of rocks under the sea
And under the earth, and of his other sons
In the country of the Gauls and at Gallipoli.
The idea of a perfect day is for the young,
Perhaps. He would have simply turned and smiled,
Looking at what he had, the boat of food,
The young man ruefully sniffing, and the lad
Too young to mind, clapping him on the back...

A day to keep, especially for the lad
Who would intercept a letter at the ferry
About this brother's wound, from a poor Sassenach
Who heard him cry in the shell-hole, saw his spine
Exposed like a sardine's, and had to hear
His guessed-at final words and possibly kill him,
Like someone else's favourite dog or horse –

Another picture saved for seventy years.

A Pearl Necklace

fert Britannia aurum . . . gignit et Oceanus margarita
Tacitus, *De Vita Agricolae* 12

Tacitus married a nameless girl from Wroxeter –
I think, a farmer's daughter –
and became interested in our islands.
In his book about her father
he says that Ocean here
breeds pearls – admittedly
subfusca ac liventia –
but even that strains the credulity
of his learned Scottish commentator.

If I could say a word to them
(both dead), after an encomium
on their amusing book, I'd murmur,
"My father also married a farmer's daughter,
and gave her a necklace of those pearls
from a salmon river in the Highlands –
he came from there and used to gather
oysters from the brackish water
as well as leapers from the sweet.

That circle of mollusc kidney-stones,
only just big enough to thread,
was the sort of thing a little
dirty-legged Gaelic-speaking girl
might make and wear, herding the cattle.
It barely went round my mother's neck –
and felt like wearing a toy
last played with in the neolithic.
She gladly handed it on
to my wife Barbara who is learning Greek."

Some Scottish Music

Behind the voices of di Stefano
And Callas, others sing. I seem to hear
In the same stream an earlier *Lucia*
Filling another room with love and woe.

The fire, the sons, their parents smell of peat,
The fume of family; their chairs scrape, on flags
Awkwardly covered with the skins of stags;
Is the wax cylinder too near the heat?

The sextet or the summers of their glen
Stored up and now released affect their eyes:
They look at nothing for a moment.

Then
The eldest son rewinds his phonograph
And plays the overture. To their surprise
The dog howls at the piccolo.

How they laugh,
The woman and her men! – the waterfall
Frozen, the snow unmarked for miles around,
The sea-loch and the hills of Sutherland, all
Invisible behind Italian sound.

Bless the Bed that I Lie On

i.m. Marion Elliot, née Margaret Stewart (Nedd, 1859 - Lochmore, 1955)

The history of this blanket's partly known:
You made it - starting not from yarn but wool
Sheared perhaps from a known sheep in Glencoul,
And lichen, from the ultrabasic stone.

But is it older than your grandson? – made
Before your blindness, when you were a wife,
In the middle of your long pseudonymous life?
Or in my teens, when you were half a shade?

Is it your photograph I recall, or you,
In black against a white wall in the sun
Turning your wheel?

I'd like to think you spun
And dyed and wove my blanket in Glendhu,
Still in the drystone park like paradise
In summer

– even that it kept you warm
That night beside your husband's mortal form,
Waiting together for the sun to rise.

The Last Day of Marriage

You told my mother your old husband died
In the small house in the dark glen, Glendhu;
That no one there could lay him out but you;
And your one place to sleep was by his side,
As if the double bed were still your bed.

And now your son's that age, I think my mother
(Foreseeing widowhood) fears such another
Dissolving night beside the newly dead.

The hours of little sleep at either end
Of marriage are too secret to be told;
The grandson and the son must not pretend
To understand the silence of the old.
I try to reach across those thirty years
With comfort: the dumb comfort of a kiss
Suddenly given can relieve those fears –

But how I wish that we could speak of this.

Speak to Me

"Telling the stones", the Highland formula says.
And did you? I imagined your slow walk
At sunset, to a circle; difficult talk
In Gaelic to the stony witnesses;
Fearing your troubles might leak out to islands
And rocks and lochs that pick up every sound...

But you meant squares like this, tame Christian ground
Where the dead exercise their gift of silence –
Good listeners, will you never speak again?

We think we go unanswered. In old age
We might hear. Then I'll make the pilgrimage
By Maldie to your house in the black glen –
There you might murmur to me what you know;
If I refilled the stony dairy shelves
With bowls of milk and cream, the ancient selves
Might join in that communicating glow?

III

Talking Back
(1982)

Talking to Horace

for John Milner

"I wonder what it's like at parties now?"

You'd still hear the familiar human row,
The sound of egos belling, face to face,
As if competing in a market-place
To sell themselves; but louder, for we walk
Or stand to drink, avoiding general talk –
A mob, you'd say, but in its Sabbath best.
I think you'd see that, though we'd not be dressed
In white like you, or uniformed by class.
Also, we "smoke": a dried-up herb – not grass –
Held in a paper tube, burnt and breathed in,
To give a swooning sense of harmless sin.
Then, you'd see ladies drinking with us; and
No slaves (none of your coupling on demand).

"Sad loss!"

Well!

You'll be wondering, no doubt,
What Britons ("fierce to guests") could talk about.

"You're *British!*"

Yes, and *sapiens* like you –
That's what two thousand years of thought can do.
Thus, at a northern house the other night
You were named twice. You're famous still all right,
Although your golden mean has disappeared
Like Croesus' gold . . . and Aristotle's beard.

Diffugere nives, but English thaws
Can't make our snow run off as fast as yours,
Even in March. So we were cold and late
Coming to toast a friend's new Doctorate.
(The belly, still, to honour a full head,
Calls in some friendly bellies to be fed.)
But first, with glass in hand, we talk: on pets,

Children, the cost of fluoride and vets,
Preoccupations of a family
That fret us all, now everyone is free;
Meanwhile our Doctor's younger son aged three's
Padding round barefoot, head above our knees:
We shuffle carefully, in case his nose
Catches some treasure guarded by our clothes;
The owner, by the fire, plays the male game
Of warm-your-breeches at the naked flame:
A separated viscountess; her man
And she would strike you as Italian –
I'd have said, "Well-off artist," by her looks.

Nice paintings, but no chance to see the books:
Oh, lucky painters, who without offence
Can scan your art at sociable events!

I met a "farmer's wife" and asked her how
They farmed: she looked too frail to wield a plough...
They live by breeding Morgans (horses): she
Was born (like them) beyond the Atlantic Sea.
"I too" – but it was dinner-time, before
I could say "crossed that Ocean – in the War."

Eating by candle-light (but on a chair)
At tables forming three sides of a square –
Arrayed like Romans for attacking food –
I never thought of you, it was so good.
I forget all my pretty neighbours said,
But – would our menu please the gourmet dead?

"Go on!"

We've found some new things, dear old-timer,
Since you concocted *Catius' eating primer:*

A fat red squashy vegetable, nice
Chopped up with lettuce, vinegar, oil and rice –
Love-apples – what your Sabine farmer calls
"Apples of gold" or "Atalanta's balls";
Then, a gold berry, *Hesperidium*
(But found in India), whipped into a scum

With cream (from cows, not goats) and "sugar" (honey
Would do), and gelatine (it wasn't runny);
But no more novel plants – you mustn't think
Us holus-bolus vegetarians: pink
Salted pork, sausage, cold domestic birds
(Do you recall the tastes, or just the words?)
And wine, still drunk (and drunk in every land,
Though one Arabian god has had it banned).

Dimmed by this meal we staggered up for hot
Drinks in the hallway. Some could dance; I, not.
The next thing I remember is a thin
Girl who'd begun a thesis on Dupin
And Labrunie, two Gauls well-known to Fame
(Though, like Ulysses, under a false name)
And even (she was hoping) to each other;
This was on top of being (twice) a mother.
I'd asked her what she did! – What do *I* "do"?,
I thought (as fond of sleep and books as you).
Luckily then, to save me from self-blame,
A tall Pict (with a Jewish poet's name –
And not tattooed!), one of our best Horatians,
Walked up to us to talk about translations.

Glazed by now as an antique painting, I
Noticed my friends stood near to catch my eye:
Time to start driving home, through all that snow.
But, as I buttoned up my coat to go,
They turned me, almost hauled me back to greet
A smiling blonde face that I "had to meet" –
I don't know why: she liked my poetry?
Something about an Open (Air?) Degree?

I liked her tomboy look – we'd met before?
(Had she a gold tooth in her lower jaw
Like mine?) Virginia? married to a man
(Like me) from an old Border reiving clan,
Now stuck in rural peace that even you'd
Find a bit deep – you'd call it solitude.

Stepping outside into the stream of night
That always seems the same, but isn't, quite –

For even heaven's not fixed, as you were told
(Your Sagittarius is bent and old),
I saw three white chairs standing by a round
White metal table on the snowy ground.
The seats, pushed back, looked dry and summery
Enough for timeless hospitality –
As if some guardian spirits had been there
Talking, and waiting to resume their care,
A moment such as our new Doctor paints:
Small man-made landscape, with invisible saints.

Were you there? Longing for your cup of blood
As Homer says?

"You'll find out, if you're good."

Talking to Bede

"You think historians must be keen to see
What followed their escape from history?
You think we can't find out? I'd rather hear
The earth described. Remind us of the Wear,
The creatures, plants and light where I began
To look around the domicile of man,
The home I only saw till I was seven."

You miss the handiworks of God, in heaven?

"That's what we all must go without; so when
You die, bring news of nature, not of men.
None of us saw enough: we lived too much
In the small range of feelings, taste and touch."

What, even you?

"You'd think not, but I still
Long for one walk across a field or hill."

The Tunstall Hills, then, limestone – did you know
More than two hundred million years ago
They were a barrier reef, at the equator?

"I knew God made the world; I did think later –
As well as man's Last Judgement being soon."

We still think that! . . . You've . . . heard about the moon?

"I know you . . . we . . . Man . . . Armstrong has been there,
Taking, as well as bait, a flask of air,
And whistled sweetly through the crystal spheres
We thought a solid mesh of ringing gears.
We got the moon wrong; but I told the tides
With some effect for sailors and their brides . . ."

Indeed you did. But how you told the tale
About the monks at sea without a sail!
Bringing down wood on rafts to Tynemouth, *they*
Were caught by wind and stream and borne away,
Till like a seabird swimming far from view
They hardly showed across the shifting blue.
Out rushed a squad of Brothers, with the Prior,
And knelt, and sent up prayers – like mortar fire!
I like your verse! – while the whole show was guyed
By local heathen from the South Shields side.
(*For good men's fates give joy to reprobates!*)
Among these Geordie rustics and their mates
Stood Cuthbert, still a boy, appalled to find
It isn't all that natural to be kind.
He tried to rouse Their Noble Savagery
To pray, and when they wouldn't, *bent his knee*
And pressed his face to earth. The wind backed east,
Or else turned turtle, for the future priest,
The rafts reached shore, and the embarrassed clods
Admitted Cuthbert's God outshone their gods.
    But surely the next tide, the evening breeze
Onshore, were not surprising prodigies
To you, but chance, coming out right for once.

"The eyes of sadness and of confidence
See the same world. You'll know whose eyes were sharp
Someday. Till then, keep looking, and don't carp."

Forgive me, Bede. The old see more; the dead,
If anything, see more than can be said.
    Do you see Durham, where your leavings lie,
Translated from the Jarrow cemetery?
– "Or rather, stolen, by a sacristan –
Aelfrid – a relic-crazy Westoe man – "
Who made you share a coffin – was that nice? –
With the shy saint whose *Life* you'd written twice.
    I went there from Pons Aelius upon Tyne
(Where Aelliots start to draw their family line?),
And saw, inside that one majestic room,
How blessed are the meek in Cuddy's tomb.
He's got two covers on his burial place:
One says, "Ricardus Heswell", to his face;
The other, laid above it, back to back,
Is meant for us: CUTHBERTUS, gold on black.
They've left his pillow with him – Oswald's head –
But now you're honoured with a separate bed.
    I stood and thought of you, the Church's light,
Your only miracle that you could write
Here in the dark of Britain, stay-at-home
Doctor, Transhumbria's answer to Jerome,
Your undivided virtue ending on
The last notes of the Gospel of St. John:
"Even the world itself could not contain
The books that should be written. Aah... *Amen."*
A life of ivory, in and out of books,
Leaving no record of your wit or looks –
The little teacher's jokes in your short course
On Writing Latin Right were never yours:
"Melissus said buttocks is feminine,
But Verrius recommends the masculine..."
"Tibiae: human shin-bones; later, flutes..."
"Riches is always plural – so is toots
(Darling – but only in the vocative)..."
"Bellus (lovely) has no comparative..."
And so on, tags I guess as old as Latin,
That sent a groan round classes Virgil sat in.
They take our feelings back to someone young
Trying the tastes of grammar on his tongue,
But not to you, I think. We can't see you
Or those you name – you didn't mean us to? –

Except: you wore your hair cut Peter's way;
In memory of the crown of thorns, you say.
Other men show us Caesar pleased at winning
A laurel crown because his hair was thinning,
Or Cleopatra's smile as Marcus took
His only catch, her kipper, off his hook,
Or, burning cakes he was supposed to cook,
The first translator of your *History* book.
You never give such details. But may I,
A disappointed customer, ask why?
I brood on how your Brothers used to make
The illuminations down by Jarrow Slake:
They drew with templates, compass and a rule –
Like pattern-lessons at an infant-school –
Or copied Bibles, inch by inch. Next door
You cut up Commentaries, and made more,
Wrote Christian elegiacs for relief,
Collected folk-tales with a saint-motif,
Learned from the authors on the library shelf
And turned into a scholar by yourself.
You never left Northumbria. But, Bede hinnie,
How could you take your geography from Pliny?

"Pax. Skinchies, Elia – Aelle – What's-your-name:
Forbear to judge. It's blasphemy to blame
The inhabitants of heaven, or of earth:
I wrote, like you, for all that I was worth."

Since Dante put you in his *Paradise*
You don't need praise; and who could criticise
The writer who rose earliest to walk
About our glittering language, still all talk?

"Pity my native stuff is lost. God knows
I worked on that despised vernacular prose..."

Strange to compose without a lexicon!

"And spell the passing words, before they're gone,
Like Adam's animals, never seen before –
And maybe soon extinct, or heard no more.
"Tell me about some animals, in fact.

Forget the Wear: thanks for your silent tact
About my birthplace and my monastery,
Despoiled by bookless raiders from the sea
And then by the original filth of man.
    "Show a consoling wonder – if you can."

Oh Bede! Your churches of St Paul's and Peter's
Are kindly kept, with services and heaters.
Through the same windows Jarrow light still falls
On surpliced cantors in their choir stalls.
There's a Musaeum: people come for miles
To see torn straps, smashed glass, nails, broken tiles,
And not to touch, relics not even yours,
For holy curiosity, not for cures.

"Yes, yes, the leavings: when they come, they see
The horrible marks of human territory
All round, where no one wants to live. What monk
Prays in these deserts of industrious junk?"

I saw a wonder on a summer's day,
Bede: I was walking on the landward way
To Lindisfarne, and found the sort of place
That puts agnostics in a state of grace,
Two rivers north of Tyne. A little breeze;
Bright ripples in the underskirts of trees;
Among the flowers on the sandy shore
Hovered an insect overlooked before
In years of scarcely looking. It was stout,
Furry and pear-shaped, with the stalk held out
To drink its nectar from a moving cup –
Two wings, so not a bee. I looked it up:
Bombylius major L. – Linnaeus too
Had seen a bee-fly in his day. Did you?
I bet, like me you'd never heard of it.
    Another first time, I watched cuckoo-spit
Nymphs blowing bubbles, and looked up at home
These things that lay their house in farts of foam:
Grown, they're the brown kind that shoot up like spray
From boots in heather or bare feet in hay:
Froghopper, typical homopteran.
    For you, Bede, dry and fresh as that dry man

Whose book connects the stages of a creature
As if there were no miracles in nature,
I hope these views from pleasant earth can cross
The barriers of years and bodily loss,
And –
"Yes. They reach me; almost with the smell
Of seasons I excluded from my cell...
Enough for now. I'll ask for a repeat
When it's your heavenly birthday."

– If we meet.

"Benedictus benedicat!"

And God bless
Your abbot Ceolfrith, patron of my Press,
And Benedict Biscop, your first abbot, who
Gathered the library that nourished you:
Tell them – they may be pleased – their fame's not large
Enough (like yours) to christen a garage,
But they're remembered where their scholar is:
You all gave names to Jarrow terraces.

John Elliot

(Auchendrain, January 29, 1844 – Glendhu, September 1928)

In the second decade of the railway age,
months after Henry James was born,
the same year as Verlaine,
my father's father arrived,
shouting across Loch Broom
while Mendelssohn's violin concerto
was being first performed.

A Gaelic childhood still,
on the mainland, with one book in it;
the Good Book was enough,
though above the barricades
the German Lazarus
worked upon more and more.
Oh grandfather, Scottish child...

As Germany was unified,
you earned your living on hills,
addict of peace and quiet
in Argyll, as Paris starved,
Verlaine eloped with his friend,
shot him and went to prison,
and taught in Lincolnshire.

In the year of *Bonheur* you married:
the line of sons began.
Verlaine wrote the poems I know so well,
the Lumières showed that train pull in,
Verlaine died, and Victoria died;
my father began to breathe
when you were fifty-seven.

Your daughter-in-law was born
with *The Ambassadors*, the first plane...
The Great War somehow began.
You and your orphaned wife from Nedd
paid two sons down; two more
fought at Gallipoli and in France;
my father helped with the Glencoul hay.

Henry James became British and died;
the war-to-end-wars came to an end;
my father went back to school,
and left the glens forever.
You watched him turn into a doctor
while Hitler was sentenced to rewrite *Mein Kampf*
and Rutherford transmuted matter.

Still never losing your temper,
you grew old in the long beard,
and died, before my parents met.
Years later, my father recognised your arm-bone
held out in the grave
at his mother's funeral:
I'd have seen you – if I'd gone.

Note: The opening stanza of 'John Elliot' alludes to the family tradition that my grandfather was born while Mendelssohn's violin concerto was receiving its first performance. After writing the poem I discovered that the tradition, fifty or sixty years old, is based on a mistake – probably encountered in George Dubourg's history of the violin (5th edition, 1878), which I have not seen.

Homeric Similes from my Autobiography

Part I

Like the fakir smiling to see the sky
as the warped lid scrapes open, and his sons
and daughters greet him ("Home on time for once!"),
and his wife waves the new best friend goodbye,
I...

As when the trumpets stop, you hear the quiet
conference of sparrows, and the captive feet
scuffing through files of neighbours down your street,
and one black mourner walks behind a chariot
looking at everything, and meets your eyes,
and passes, her pink palms chained to her thighs,
she...

Then, as on mountains when a shepherd looks
over pure world until he hears the knock
of wooden spoon on pot, and leads his flock
down through the dust to salesmen, thieves and cooks,
I...

Part II

Like the field-grey reoccupying rooms
where the earth-brown once sat, which everywhere
stink of danger (some far-off engineer
laughs in the desert at the thought of bombs)
and at the bar another language sings
the common song of people's underthings,
you and I...

But as the swift's granddaughter stops migrating
and hoop-las round a tower, and through the airs
bumpy with cooking cuts smooth arcs and spheres,
crying the hunt of insects up, and eating,
she...

Then longer than the pause when the cat's mother
enters and it runs up exchanging blows,
and they stand side by side but tail to nose
and seeing nothing each looks where the other
has walked from – till she turns to clean its fur
and it begins to feed, and blink, and purr,
we...

The Change

Unwanted days surround me,
as in a cafeteria:
congealed autumn with cold eyes,
ominous, and sloshy.

The delicious lashes and long tail
roll-calling round at dawn
bucking away or licking salty hands
have lost their personal taste:
these ladlefuls of Something
might have eaten Anything.

But further off the fauna of time still
wander uncaught,
twin days, Siamese weekends, timid mornings;
interested afternoons
catch whiffs of us thinking of them;
they hear us in the leaves beginning
our joint work on common moths,
till now completely unstudied.

The water in our mouths runs again.

A Northern Morning

It rained from dawn. The fire died in the night.
I poured hot water on some foreign leaves;
I brought the fire to life. Comfort
spread from the kitchen like a taste of chocolate
through the head-waters of a body,
accompanied by that little-water-music.
The knotted veins of the old house tremble and carry
a louder burden: the audience joining in.

People are peaceful in a world so lavish
with the ingredients of life:
the world of breakfast easy as Tahiti.
But we must leave. Head down in my new coat
I dodge to the High Street conscious of my fellows
damp and sad in their vegetable fibres.
But by the bus-stop I look up: the spring trees
exult in the downpour, radiant, clean for hours:
This is the life! This is the only life!

Homines Sapientes

Walking to work like someone's dad,
We lick at history on the way
Through sunlight and a mile of moor,
And taste the crispy modern day,

Relishing the near touch of earth:
Our toes remind themselves they tread
On something living that can grow
Lying at home all day in bed.

Pedestrianly, we overtake
The neighbours in their traffic-jam.
Pleased with our free old-fashioned gait
We laugh: "I walk; therefore I am."

But then we see a horse laid out
Motionless, swollen, on one side,
One of the ponies from the fair
That cost you such a lot to ride.

Then we see – no – it isn't dead,
Just dozing; and beside it lies
A man, his back against its back.
An arm, a tail wave off the flies.

He sucks at grasses: "He's at work
Already." And with envious looks
We pass, to your illiterates
And to my multilingual books.

Lunch-Break at the Hotspur Hotel

A sheet of glass, the whole front wall, lets in
pale cloud-reflected light on our faint grime.
The beer is clean. A strange electric lie
whispers the nunc bibendum of pub-time.
Curtains cut off all but the noblest heads
and tops of things.
                                        A man back from the south
to die, mentions a birthday or a win
and buys us all a round. I have a pie.
Kirstie comes in, who works the Norway boat.
Pictures of married daughters. She makes beds
and tends the bar. Why don't I sail across? –
she will look after (and looks straight at) me.
I buy a round now, wondering if my balls
(tightening at the seam) would play the goat
among ship-smells and salty metal walls.
We kiss, searching the inner walls (applause)
for messages of life lost in the mouth,
for bumps and grinds on lower North-Sea bunks,
years grander than our own.
                                        I leave, sadly,
and not as one who dares: as one who funks.

A Revelation

The white-haired man stands in his lonely job,
where I wash my hands. "Had lots of sun?" I say,
"You're so brown" – healthy as a body-snob –
"Is it a Spanish tan?" (Had it away
on some blond beach where buttocks and the sand
compete to warm each pensionable hand?)

"No, this year we just went to the south coast.
I'll tell you something strange..." Then quietly
(white walls have ears? some bugger's listening post?):
"Down there it gets dark sooner. It must be
an hour – the sunset – earlier than here.
I wonder why that is. Isn't it queer?"

Wonder can be like joy. Since then, all day
my mind has turned to see the age-old view
he sees. Surely he knows... The Milky Way,
the miles of nothing we are spinning through
at an angle to the planetary floor...
"Strange," I say slowly, opening the door.

Public Address

All behave quietly here.
The voices on the air
feel nothing: they are signs
for the hot listener to
thaw, like a frozen book.

The building closes in
five... means, for instance, *FREE!* –
or, if you prefer, *OUT!*

This is the dead word trick
(guess what the face is like
above those muted cords),
but it's sometimes followed
(they forget to switch off)
by private life, gratis.

The whole building listens,
sweating, to the rustle
of unmade conversation
(what will they take off next?).

Under the microscope
amoebas glide unheard,
a whisper of fluid;
here's our call, familiar
to the other species,
unknown to us: seconds
of shuffle, sentences
walking off for a piss,
half-words and hand-held jokes –
behind, to prove it's real,
the cosmos drizzling
like a rather shy clock.

Agonizing to hear
life at metronome speed –
worse than hearing your self
as you sound. A relief
when some warm finger turns
our raw universe off.

John Eateth the Book

(page heading from the Breeches Bible at Revelation 10)

"John eateth the book." I understand:
I see them daily copying their books
In a machine, imagine them at night
Stirring the powdery meal, with one slow hand,
Eager to eat the carbon and the light
So magically prepared – by other cooks.

"It shall be in thy mouth as sweet as honey,"
The angel said, but "It shall make thy womb
Bitter." The bloody vegetable ink
Brings in the aftertaste of work and money;
The Word itself glows in us, till we think
There is a goodness that may overcome.

I Know Thee Who Thou Art

Chilled in the dusty nearly level sun
Of March among the buildings, I decide
To ambush buses elsewhere; then, one comes.
(The urban gospel: "Sod's Law will provide.")

I settle by a window, in the last
Place left where one can keep on being one.
The man behind me dithers in the aisle
Among averted eyes and sprawling bums,
Looking for friends. Because I got on there
I seem the less a stranger
– till he sees
Poetry Nation glaring on my knees.

I hold it to my chest; and with a smile
Make room. It takes some courage to sit down:
He bravely does, but starts to rummage through
His plastic carriers, not to speak.

His face
Is plump and spotty, stuck with bits of hair
That don't seem his. The sky's a brilliant blue,
As everyone, except a *Poet*, says –
So I sit speechless.

In my part of town,
I just grunt, "I get off here," and squeeze past.

Saul

When we have kidney Meyerbeer –
at home now; we have not been back –
I think of you, where I first tasted it,
dark and solitary in the restaurant.
"It must be five years – more?"

We reminisced no doubt: now I recall
(as I pick up deliciously stained rice)
a poem you had shown me, in Perugia,
about English trains heard far away at night;
the mystery of painting; your terse uncle,
original of Basil Seal, in Rome
recommending islands; our American friend,
Luigi, who would come to Bonn
for Beethoven's two hundredth Geburtstagsfest,
who taught us a cheap breakfast, of raw egg
and Marsala; your lithe little half-sisters
swimming at Cosa; Amanda! and their mother
English as wild flowers; your dark curly head
not ominous then over the shaded lunch.

Soon after my first kidney Meyerbeer
I heard from someone you were found, hanging,
in your London attic. Something unbearable
had taken away the taste of everything.

Years and years later, gathering the last grains
of this saddening but often-repeated meal,
I remember my room in the Via Antenori:
wakening there in the dark to flash after flash –
not lightning but a little glowing fly:
it floated round the walls, another life.

There is always something to be happy with?

Seeing You in a Documentary

People pass on the boring promenade
not looking round, until your face up there
closer and closer turns to the camera,
as if you knew, that grey uncertain day,
the sight of you would travel, miles and years,
with no forbidden writing and no stamp,
to where my disbelieving face, half here
after another crisis, turns and sees
its second wife dissolve before its eyes,
dark glasses brutally expressionless.

To My Son Aged Ten

The Sunday noises of TV next door
remind the old in their last home – and me –
of the tradition, a world of hymns:
a nation singing, recovering from a war,
lives growing up like plants to definite heights,
at a botanical speed: how we looked forward
to being grown-up! You, complete already,
lie back reading among the foreign colours
(the cotton carpet from Baghdad). And I:
every evening is different; will I ever
see you like this again? My ghost groans
adding here to the places it must haunt.
I weep behind my hand in sympathy.

House-Rules I: Reading

Among the white walls we read quietly.
The rugs beam up unnoticed.
We try not to read out the bits we like:

There you are swimming on your back in some dark lake
squinting with wet eyes at some friendly constellation
when this madman begins skimming out coloured stones.

The beautiful sofa of my cell
gets solitary, with you over there.
Life pours away, a whisky tap left on:

Here I am treading water out of sight of land
when up foams someone wearing nothing, in her hand
some bread and butter and the mermaids' local paper.

House-Rules II: Lights

Taking all armour off
taking off all protection
you come to me, carrying
like something delicate in a paper bag
yourself in your skin.

Air moves out of the way:
a bow wave must be coming
but I feel nothing,
until the warmth, the comfortable circles
of marriage, lie down
beside my open palm.
Strange permission, of nakedness together:
like being alone, not modest, uneventful
among the laws that cannot be repealed.
Lights off (our light); and reconvene
the interrupted lifetime of our bodies.

After, the aboriginal cold
creeps in under the clothes: Jack Frost
master of all
putting his finger on our brows and necks,
who will outlast even *Amoeba proteus*
now celebrating somewhere with his clone
his three thousand millionth birthday.

A Touch of Death

Strange fingers woke me, fumbling at my brow.
My rooms were near a roof. I thought: Somehow
Someone's got in. The cold hand hit my nose.
Naked between the freezing sheets, I froze.
Then... nothing happened. I became aware
Horribly slowly no one else was there:
Quite dark, but you could sense across the floor
The usual wooden quadrupeds, no more.
Was it a corpse's hand, put in my bed
By my best friend, who's studying the dead?
Surely he'd not do that... The arm felt grey,
Somehow, and yielding, in a foul soft way.
It didn't smell, though. Feeling worse, and colder,
I ran my left hand up it to the shoulder,
Expecting torn-out strings, a bulb of bone,
And wetness. Worst of all, it was my own –
I'd two right arms: one, warm beneath my head
And pillow, there; and this, cold, slack, and... dead?
I tried to touch the real one where I knew
It must be, but my fingers went straight through.
All the sensations of my arm lay there
In order, like a well-lit thoroughfare,
But not the arm. My soul is breaking free,
I thought: I'll lose the arm. I might lose me!
I grabbed the dead thing. It was powerless.
I rubbed the muscles, stroked and tried to press
The blood along, like air in a balloon,
But nothing made it feel. It would die soon,
If it weren't dead already. Then I thought:

If I could swing it round, it might get caught
As it goes through its image. Can you fit
Your arm back in the space that matches it?
The elbows fused together as they met,
The wrists and knuckles too – a perfect set.
And even when I moved them on, they stayed
United as they'd been since they were made.
I felt the rushing happiness of a boy
Who's found the key he needs to wind his toy.
I slept then, I suppose. I don't recall.

You'll keep this quiet, won't you? After all,
Who'd ever shake this hand – with which I write –
Knowing it died and met its ghost one night?

Allah Akbar: Winter: A.H. 1344

When Shiraz was Shiraz, Cairo was one of its suburbs
Persian Proverb

Outside the city, *sahra*: miles of dust.
But you heard lions roaring: all night long
The dark blue lid was filled with this wrong noise.
"They don't have lions here! It can't be lions!"
An Indian circus . . . with the handsomest audience:
I sat amazed among the Ghashghai nomads.

December: in a taxi, with a pot,
I'd bring lunch home (the Garden of the Sheikh,
With exhibitions of the kinds of leaf) –
A twist of sumac dust, a yolk of egg
And yoghurt, rice, kabab, Islamic beer:
The unexpected happiness of meals . . .

Across the road (they say) the King of Kings
Drained off the blood that disagreed with him;
Around the corner someone generous
Gave goods away (just breaking someone else);
At our gate a beggar couple propped a child
Hired by the hour and drugged to look like death.

Going to work, I'd stop a taxi, shouting
"Literature", and if he shook his head, get in.
Wildly, as if he rode a horse, he'd drive me
To the Knowing-Place of Courtesies – House of Sin,
Said one (because the students never wore
Those long dark veils sprinkled with tiny flowers).

One day you told our servant I'd invited
Seven monkeys to dinner: "Get a pound
Of sheep's ears." O, to be a foreigner!
The week it rained I went one afternoon
To bargain at the *baazaar*. Dim and quiet;
I met a man who taught me how to play.

He sat down and gave me *chai*: Was I
From Englistan? I lived in . . . ? "Bagh-e-Sheikh."
Ah, I spoke Farsi. Yes, he had a fine
Kettle (a tinny thing) for ten tomans . . .
"Amrika-y nistam, vali Englis."
Well, perhaps eight? "I wanted a less fine . . ."

We spoke. His bearded face laughed into mine.
We drank another cup. More happiness
At sitting in the world exchanging words
(And goods) – the envy of all travellers,
Who, where the mountain road displays Shiraz,
Kneel in the dust in tears: Allah is great!

Recalling the Goddess: Spring: A.H. 1345

The statue of Shapur . . . at the mouth of a cave three miles up the valley . . . climb of 600 feet . . . perpendicular, and I stuck . . . Mr Hyde carved his name on it in 1821 . . . swim in the river . . .

Robert Byron, *The Road to Oxiana*

"When I was at Beal . . . the one-armed bandits . . ."
"When I
was . . . took a taxi . . . tyres blew out three times . . .
kept a good lookout . . . bandits, the nurse said . . .
they were ten years younger – finally I gave up . . .

I thought I'd die . . . the cave . . . nothing to drink
but a bottle of warm vodka . . ."
                                        When I went,
we got off where the old (Sassanian) road
angles down rocks to the plain of Kazerun.
The tea-house; the carved rock; a man pissed, squatting.
There, the fire-temples and the heat: I too
felt my age – L. was obsessed by it.

Among the orange-blossom streets we found
a hotel: and after eating, in the moonlight
saw some abandoned houses sudden as bomb-sites,
being sanded down by time. Smooth brown tiles
by the four beds in our room, instead of Bibles,
to touch your forehead on when bent to pray.
They slept with their faces under the quilt, feet bared.
(I dreamt of you – the act of population.)

In the morning, soft-boiled seed of hens, tea, bread.
Now I have learned to wipe my arse with water.
Cold and early, swinging into the truck,
with labourers – what can you say? – we smiled
at the handsome faces, ashamed of watches and travel.
A goat, kicked, under the seat. My back!
We passed the lines like bomb-holes in the desert
(a seventh of the able-bodied men
go down there every day, shepherds of water).

Skirting the mountains. Finally, Bishapur:
the road in a gully; red dust; a green tea-house;
man with a withered arm, proud of his glasses:
"My cigarette is silent. Have you light?"

We climbed to Shapur's castle. By the edge
of the red cliff in the soft stone we found
the place cut for him: he would face the dawn:
from below you'd have seen the crowd of hungry birds.
"It's really a bed" – L. got in – "with a new twist
to getting out the wrong side in the morning."
The clear air stretches out for miles, forever,
with the descendants of those birds still wheeling
unfed over their dry and tasty empire.

Goats and nomads all over the valley,
the overlapping kingdom that goes back
earlier than cities, the first kings of kings.

Below in stone Valerian kneels to Shapur.
When *he* died, he was stuffed and carried round.
Water is wearing the great relief away:
was it dangerous to walk barefoot down the stream?

Later, in the ruins (a criticised excavation)
we called on Anahita, goddess of water
who sings both day and night. We had watched in silence
the weavers in the tent; I had reached the cave;
I had seen the fallen statue – no warm vodka –
but plagued by a quotation from myself:
"not to be absent is the prayer of skin."

The next day we went on, losing height, praying
at every turn in the deep dust, the driver
leading our chant, past strings of climbing camels
to the lovely wooden decors of the coast.

Genius for openings in walls. Verandahs.
Dhows. The forbidden island. Sinbad's gulf
and Milton's. A seal from Susa.
                                        And flew back,
like M., but with no sharks under our arms,
To the family, the mulberry tree, the wall named Jim.

The Aegean: Summer: 493 B.C.

"...took easily the islands off the mainland, Chios and Lesbos and Tenedos."
Herodotus, *History* 6.31

There is something strange about so much blue.
And I cannot believe it has no edge:
it has the feel of this side of a cliff.
But it seems the fishermen say blue just goes on,
further and further. But it must run out
somewhere: so must the land. It does in islands,
so I suppose the mainland is an island.

Anyway we are here, conquering the world.
Travelling it would be enough for me:
but it also has to be kept. That's harder.
We have beaten their soldiers but these people
won't accept that – perhaps I wouldn't either –
so we have exercises like today's.

Daryush sent us to the island there –
I can see it from this table – peacefully
recovering, giving back the sun its heat –
to net and decimate the islanders.
This morning hand in hand and joining on
so as to cover the ground from coast to coast
– it was like a game; everyone was from Fars –
we walked across it letting them through the net
but quietly killing every tenth. The counting
was done by me for our section, and Farhad
killed them. I did the best I could to make it happen
so we killed not just men or not just women
but children too, to thin them equally,
so that each family would remember us,
but Farhad said he was tired of killing women –
and then we found a young one in a field.
Farhad said he couldn't – it would be like
spitting on food or pissing on the Fire.
He made her stay with him; took an old man
instead; but then, after a baby and a boy,
said he was too exhausted to go on.
We let him go – we could see the girl was lovely.

It's been a hard day. We are tired, and some
were seasick coming back.
They're calling me –
The scream was Farhad. As we should have thought
(but they had been trying to talk for hours and hours)
she killed him: bit his shame off, stuck a knife
under his naked ribs. I had to stop them
from killing her in turn. That is not right.

Perhaps it is her beauty and not justice
that made me save her, but I made them wait
for the Commander. Then when Daryush came
he just gave her to me: "He was your brother."

Mother, I can't. I don't know what to do.

A Farangi Broadens His Mind: Autumn: A.H. 1345

"He that travels in the Highlands may easily saturate his soul with intelligence, if he will acquiesce in the first account."

Samuel Johnson, *Journey to the Western Isles of Scotland*

First the landscape was green, with pigeon towers,
like windmills without sails, hidden in trees
in the shallow vale (no river could be seen),
and the road ran among fields of bright young wheat.
Not a bad road, but soon it turned from black
to the same brown as everything in sight,
not boring brown but shades of buff and grey,
old battlefields of botany, rock, and drought:
not a desert – the driver doesn't pause
to pray for safety in this merely waterless place.

Occasional man on a camel in the distance.

After an hour of delicately scanning
these miles of absent lake in powder form
I had to explain myself across the aisle
in shouts, to a teacher who couldn't understand
travelling for pleasure. So we gave up that,

and I asked about the little roadside cairns:
what could these pyramids of twenty stones
signify? He was full of explanations:
They put them up to mark the road. "But, please,
excuse me, we can see the road already."
It's for the winter, when because of rain
the road's a river. "But can't they see the river?"
The snow conceals it all. "The stones too, no?
And still the road being lower" (using hands)
"than what it goes through shows itself far better
than a few stones."
                                        Then (as I'd long been hoping)
we passed a man kneeling in the great plain
to make a cairn, his folded coat beside him.
"Look, what's he doing?" *Who? I did not see.*
In the evening light I couldn't make him see
the dusty dwindling peasant.
                                                  Far from home
at nightfall people heap up stones for nothing.

Then through the window, as he stared at me,
I saw two people praying with the sun
lengthening shadows down the orange slope,
their coats beside them: and they faced two cairns.

"Look, it's a guide for praying towards Mecca!"
Again he missed them. And polite as ever,
The Holy City is another way
and nobody needed stones to pray toward it –
disgraceful thought! We didn't speak again:
outsiders are not serious human beings.
How could they understand or behave well?
No wonder they have to travel to learn wisdom.

Getting off, I bowed, my hand across my heart.
Hastily he did too. *And God protect.*

My Country 'Tis of Thee (1940-45)

in memory of Esther M. King

O my America, you are so full,
I'm always having to repack you. Like
A mother, wanting space inside myself,
I shove my pre-war Katzenjammer Kids
Under my first American bed (late '40),
And linger over one of me, eleven,
In a baseball tree, batting the apples out,
And ("The Financial Lesson") pedalling home
Along Lake Worth at dusk, a Chinese fall
Cascading in one hand: a wealthy man
Stops me and makes me sell it for a profit.

Delicious amateur America,
Favourite museum, where so many things
Bear the wrong labels or are unexplained,
And everything's earlier than the atom bomb –
I've something to donate. Let's throw away
"Sitting in Palm Beach in the Messerschmitt
In the spring of 1941" – will that
Clear out enough? – or this, the whitewashed room
In the empty house, with dead leaves on the floor
And the receiver dangling, with Chicago
Dead at the other end (some crook had lived here)?

I'll keep the cottonmouths (shot with a B.B. gun);
The yellow-zeppelin kumquats and tummaytoes;
Baudelaire, Elinor Wylie, Frank L. Baum
(All in the attic); L.S.M.F.T.! –
O my America! This time I've brought
Not some caricature from your enemies,
Not a line of verse, or tale of tasteless bread
And policy, but a little mended finger:
Thanks to a rubber-band and safety-pin
(*Kleinert's Traction*, from Tennessee), my hands,
Hands anywhere, can applaud again; or fight.

The Latitudes of Home

Here I read Biggles; in this chair, *Ulysses;*
Here I watched sperm wriggle across a slide
Slower and slower as their element dried;
In this back corridor I gave secret kisses
To tins of sweet milk, other people's blisses;
Ironed on this table; underneath it tried
To find the pleasure grown-ups used to hide;
And here faced east for several thousand pisses.

Meanwhile my father earned the means of life
At this thin desk; my mother was his wife;
The cost of living rose each dreamy year
Till now: his surgeon, gratis, lifts a knife
And starts to cut him; and I think with fear
Till now I never wrote a poem here.

The Last British Battle

for Pauline Dower

Your uncle, the hard-walking historian,
Described the place (trying to please his father):
Drummossie Moor lay quiet, as in shock;
To the south, beyond the neolithic circle,
Some navvies built a viaduct; and north
Across the firth, within an outstretched arm,
The gentle Highland mountains turned their back
On Highlanders being butchered through this heather,
The haze of distance in the blur of death.

My Stewart ancestor was there, that April,
Killing his man perhaps, that personal way;
Wounded, escaped the field and hid alone
Some nights; then, giving up his former life,
Made for the Northern Lights, the rocky farm,
The seaweed harvest, and a Gaelic wife –
A happier ending than his bonnie prince
Would have in Rome, prime victim of Drambuie,
Unable to give up the old pretence.

At Saxtead Green

So we climbed the broad steps into the mill.
It was quiet, with an insecticidal smell,
not old-fashioned at all, unlike the levers,
and loops of thong, and wooden chutes and bags
which spread their fainter fumes among oiled cogs
and grinding wheels under new wooden covers.

The two of us tried to see how the power
flowed down these catching circles through the floor
into the stone, while the boys had to climb
and pull at bars and ropes, and worry us
with cries and sounds of falling. So you made peace,
waived understanding, and left with one of them.

Then Willy pulled a string, and the whole mill
began to shake, obeying some unheard call
with coupled forces, which it seemed would smash
the precious antique parts – *we'll both be killed!* –
the runaway air-turned-iron uncontrolled
threw round the creaking works in a thunderous rush.

Somehow I kept bare hands from intervening
and dragged us safely out into the evening,
where on a bench the guardian still sat
stroking his dog, and you admiringly
watched the sails turn: it was the wind, not Willy,
rising a little, that had caused all that.

I almost broke their toy, I almost had
thousands to pay, one of us might be dead...
still churned inside me. Knowing it was not
an accident but a coincidence
didn't much help: *so the mistaken sense*
could throw me into gear without a thought...

Horrible when the deep machine takes over:-
puking on terra firma, the land-lover
helpless because a face has come or gone.
You had to drive us home, so I was free
to look back at the great sails emptily
turning. Better worked idly than not run.

On Holiday

Shut in their legendary summer
as real as mine
with golden light common to both
the boys run

quiet as night-bound lives that zoos
shift onto days.
Seeming to avoid our eyes, to hear
no urban voice,

they ignore the pale inquisitive grown-ups
trapped and fretting
through the same hours, on the far side
of something –

thoughts like shop-windows standing between
us and our ease,
or like a surface holding back
fish from flies,

till, going down to the North Tyne
for a starry piss,
I find I'm not discreetly drizzling
into the grass

but pattering on great leaves like rhubarb:
what I shatter
under the dark near-African trees
doubled in water

is not the composure of a scene
and a man,
but silence, the one shield at night.
Frightened, I hurry in.

Ingredients of a Sleepless Night in Wales

Lager from Wrecsam; heard over the phone
– words posted directly down the ear –
of a friend's death by drowning (the North Sea
with sun on it last Monday); wading back
to bed through fields of dew (not whispering now)
among hills ennobled by the sun's last rays;
delivering David's message from the pub
like a speech (about calves) to a kitchen full of folk;
tea; conversation (two women more than men);
and trying to tell by noses who is whose;
hearing (from bed) their parting stories – how
farmers can laugh, how much they can allude to! –
and then the noises of the immature night:
a shot at half-past twelve, a little later
repeated jerks at a fence (somebody wounded?
Morse? should I get up?), the unsleepy bed
in the next room, with healthy little children
visiting their healthy parents in the hot dark.

But how well you feel in the morning – light unpacks
the daily present; swallows on the wire
practise turning to face the other way;
skin in the sheets still able to imagine
everything suddenly wrenched out in the sea.

After Heavenfield

Trailing our battle-perfumes, we fall down
to the undusted stream, and stick our blades
into the muscling water. The cold flow
bears off our weariness as well. We hear
the rush of elements, and look round again:
"God, what a cut!" "There's something in your beard."
And thinking of our families and the wives
of those we buried on the hill, we dip
our helmets for a drink, and throw the rest
at friends, liquid that sparkles in the air

and glows on backs. We shout: We won! We won!
and bare-arsed in the sun, we share the bread
on crumbling stones, and brush the flies away,
and eat in silence, as the morning goes.

Trying to Read Outdoors

The seeds of rose-bay willow-herb float down,
swirling in silence on the streams of air
above the noisy river. Now and then
a leaf is softly turned, turned back again,
the silky scholarship of summer.

Still more insects, golden after lunch,
prick out the turbulence. Some draw bright lines
across a shadow; most, in fuzzy schools,
drift on a current, intermingling files,
or hit the water, race their engines,

and vanish, struggling, eastwards. I am old
compared with them and what I lean against,
thinking about the endless lapse of fluid;
but their kind got here first. We share the world
a little, equally entranced

by sunlight: a biography of rain
is someone else's, and my rowan tree,
air-sick or earth-sick, but outliving man,
holds up its prehistoric feast again –
to the dark birds of the next century.

Alexandrines for Livy

In Livy's wonderful history of the city
From its foundation, there's just the triangular ball
Out in the water, and the leg, its famous boil
Pulsating by the knee. Everywhere else is misty,

At first: behind thick cloud Aeschylus sweats and thumbs
His worn-out sword; a nameless Indian invents chess;
Three Aztec prisoners can't sleep; early forms of us
Lose their virginity, their axes, querns and combs.

But here, already focused, round the consuls' tent
Plebeian faces, deafened in their helmets, lean
To the great argument: will their centurion,
Named Marcus Flavoleius, call a strike, and end

The future empire? We are stirred; but they don't know
There are a hundred volumes someone's got to fill.
For Christ's sake, on the horizon Greece is visible.
Won't there be panning shots of elephants and snow?

Won't there be Livy? Sitting here and looking down
We see his book hauled up in jerks through layers of time
Like Simeon Stylites' lunch, and feel the column
Of history trembling now – as it has always done.

Epistle to an Alien

Here in my kitchen, conducted through a continuous sunshine
by the grandfather clock, with cadenzas from an old fridge,
I am picking an argument, just for the sake of music,
out of the night behind tongues, our black artesian cortex,
with the unanswerable dead, the language-hunter and trainer,
Auden, who put his head in the mouths of dictionaries so well
we were no longer amazed, and some had forgotten to read him.

Dear poet, dearer now you are silent as Caesar and Stalin
than when your atoms made sense and your molecules
autographed fly-leaves,
why (when you wrote with cousinly sorrow of daily disasters
suffered by creatures who cultivated your skin) did you think so
ill of the Insects? You wrote, *What Saint made a friend of a roach or
preached to an ant-hill?* It happens there was such a moment; each
evening
in a Greek jail one man in solitary rolled up his shirt-sleeves
for his three thirsty friends, mosquitos, who would remember
at a concurrence of light and dust and odours of cooking
George Mangakis, land among hairs, and drink from the runway.
They gave him what friends give: times and reasons for meeting,
bar-lines and rests, a structure, occasional hints of a theme-song.
When he was moved to another cell, he missed them. They
couldn't
find him.

One instance can, and this does, falsify theories:
breaks in the filament. But the lighting-threads in a poem
carry just part of its current; they lie like yesterday's dinner
seen through the dome of a jelly-fish, hazily being digested.
Feeling jumps over the gaps. Your poem (irregular ending
and all) has what we ask of poems here in the cosmos:
something we want to learn, a game to play over and over,
flaws in the rules being only a Muse-given pause for refreshments.

In the disordered atmospherics of nowhere it must seem
quite dissolved though, like everything made by our thought
and our bodies
(even replacements we so humanly, vainly, engender) –
like yourself, Auden, now, who seeing the too-unemphatic
face of truth realise *what we must never become.*

Straightening out Virgil

caeruleos implexae crinibus anguis
Eumenides

Georgics IV. 482-3

As Orpheus sang, the very halls of Hell
And inmost sculleries yielded to the spell;
And the Eumenides stood stock-still there,
Those dark blue snakes tight-knotted in *their hair.*

The Saxons were destroying Roman Britain
As our best manuscript of this was written:
In rustic capitals IMPLEXAE *twined*
Coils among tresses for the reader's mind.
One day an ancient hand, perhaps the paw
Of Apronianus (consul 494,
The owner), in a brainwave made it better
Than Virgil had, by taking out one letter –
IMPEXAE: Furies that you mesmerise
Must get their *uncombed* serpents in their eyes.

Another (Rustic is as Rustic does)
Conceived it was the same – INNEXAE – as
In *Aeneid* VI: 'Great! The Eumenides,
In hair*nets* made of sea-green vipers, freeze.'
And all the learned men of Charlemagne
Nod, "Yes – except, AMPLEXAE: they *contain*
Their hypnotising wig of snakes with . . . hair.'

Ixion's wheel stops in the windless air,
Cerberus' muzzles gape and gape and gape;
And going back he's *managed to escape*
With his Eurydice returned again,
When . . .

A Warning to Wordsworth: or, the Lay-Detector Rampant

...the intensity of emotion expressed in the "Lucy poems" occurs elsewhere in Wordsworth's poetry of the period only in those poems involving Dorothy and, therefore...she becomes the leading candidate for the original of Lucy. This conclusion leads logically...(etc. etc. etc.)

Donald H. Reiman *T.L.S.* Nov.1, 1974

Dear William, watch it: he can read your pulse,
but Wasserman-tests all your waters first –
'Tis three foot long, two wide' is something else,
and mirrored mountains make him fear the worst.

'Proteus rising' (shades of urethritis!)
leads on to London's sweetly gliding pee,
but Venice has the best claim to excite us:
'She must espouse the everlasting Sea.'

Can he declare you treated as a wife
the unvisited City (ooh! its Grand Canal!)?
'The dreary intercourse of daily life'
meant no-holds-barred to a Romantic gal?

And what went on in Davy Jones's locker
when she encountered her drowned sailor-brother?
Something no doubt not quite according to Cocker-
mouth standards of a kiss or bit of other.

Be warned then, though perhaps it doesn't matter
if hygroscopic poets are abused
or glotterotic critics merely flatter:
soon all are far more deeply interfused.

Reply to a Painter

'Our stuff may not be pretty,
but at least we've got a Muse.'
Choerilus of Iasus (*Letter to Apelles*, c.325 B.C.)

An art of peaceful objects! You make things
From bits of world, possessions that we keep
In rooms, or graves, useful like wedding-rings,
Symbols to guard, and polish, dust, or sweep.
But poems aren't the paper, cloth, stone, wood.
They're found between the senses and the pulse,
In dark pink catchment areas where blood
Washes the words of men and animals.
They replicate: the copies are as new.
We carry them invisibly. They lie
Unmelted in the mouth through all we do,
A hundred light as one; and when we die,
They sweeten, incorrupt, some younger head:
The immortal public property of the dead.

Finishing Off a Book

Open-mouthed, the poems look up like fish
from the carpet where they lie, scattered,
hungry for juicy readers.

I remember a valley where distributed sheep
all turned and stared at me:
My God! a guest without a tie!

How will I round them up? A sheep-dog-fish?
A liquid whistle stirs nothing
but dust in my extra-marital room.

I assert myself: I'll sort you!
Finally I do, parting families,
twins, friends of the class of '71.

And grow cold to them: schools, flocks,
something to sell. Something to give:
something to give away?

Dedications! tracks of a doubled life,
names that inspire creative questions
between the sheets, in the pocket-money queue!

And books have names: not Rex, not Daisy –
Airs of Return, Heat Transfer in Packed Beds,
The Skin is the Best Part, Contentions...

Kiss the man goodbye.

IV

from Contentions (1977)

The Consolations of Natural Philosophy

Always when there seems nothing left to do
there will be people, and the world, to view:
spectator-pleasures. And forget we know
the audience dies before the end of the show.

The World

You speak of getting away
to an anonymous place
not visited by fame –
as if you could avoid them,
cultural syllables,
brand-names of peoples,
in some neutral landscape
immune to aesthetics and hope.

Water, the same old sound,
a stream, a fall, a pool,
would seem the same all over:
sensations of forever,
being outlived both ways
by an element fashionless
though lapsing, drinkable
but unhistorical.

But the views made by its laws
(never revised or repealed)
are dotted with houses, or hills
reformed by pitmen or pastorals,
under Roman constellations.
Remember the confluence
of Japan and Rhineland spas
meeting at High Force:

where we felt wrongly dressed
on the path with a rustic rail
in the mid-Victorian wood
and the Pre-Raphaelite Brotherhood
had designed a feathery downpour
fused with a self-conscious roar
to the fierce weight at its foot
(every third wavelet white).

It's no good thinking you
can see the vain unknown:
even electrons appear
to sport in period air –
cloud-chamber photographs,
permanent waves, mass graves.
We have seen so much we see
just styles of history.

The untouched universe
is a vision of the young,
who tasting each other taste
pure other unrehearsed –
which is not to say our tasting
for the pure sake of tasting
is without awe and dangers:
who is friends with the universe?

Visiting the Tomb of Hafiz

Under your alabaster the light is golden,
Its shadows your own poems,
And the insoluble has been dissolved:
You are not separated from anything;
There are no cells in your particular world.

Here we have skins, each one with its own sweetness,
Liquors finite and lonely,
On which we live, trembling with surface-choices.
And the sun dries our world of dew: it threatens
The distant evaporation of a friend.

Hafiz, she is my element; speak for me
To the smooth laws of tension;
Preserve our field, where we are good alone,
And even the arts of man are small diversions
From the look of eyes we shall not see for years.

On Running into Old Friends in Somebody's Novel

(viz., Richard G. Stern's *Europe, or, Up and down with Baggish and Schreiber*, published New York, 1961)

Inside the margins of a book
through the screen doors of ink
you find yourself among explained people,
whom you imagine from one clue, or two,
people you cannot bore or smell,
who will not love you or seduce your friend.
They have names out of telephone books –
Baggish and Schreiber –
but of course they are not real.

How strange then
on a train in there
to meet someone you know:
one who remembers moonlight on two faces –
enough to read a face by
if old enough to read –
and hesitating near the shadow;
and that one's voice; that dog, that awful dog;
and him, the man without a neck,
whose grandfather invented
telephone insulators.
There they all are, characters, helpless now,
but looking round at the compartment door
when Baggish enters,
as if they could sense me,
invisible but behind his back,
a recognisable reader.

And then, how strange for them, now –
but maybe they're all dead –
to read these lines, to feel those days again:
Jocrisse, the burnt mountains,
the mysterious German gardener,
Caval-en-l'air, the dead snake in my bed,
the weeks of cherry-blossom-exclamation!

So afterwards, on your way to Austria,
for the cheap shoes,
you must have met this novelist on your train,
while I met Giuliana and the Sheriff.

Perhaps if you read this you'll write me
offering as you did before, a job –
teaching (a great-great-grandson, this time)
Latin and algebra.

Thank God I'm real only –
at least I can ignore a letter,
put a frame round it, hang it up
without answering: but you,
whenever I feel like looking,
remain there in that book,
rocking along in the train for me to stare at;
outside, the mountains of 1951.

The Sense of Theft

Sometimes, the sadness of our variation,
We find clear water, pleasure on a face,
Thick red fruit at the end of our first garden
In the wet grass, the innocent, the early,
The oldest colours against naked legs,
And come back toward midday with a dry
Grin fixing slowly round our teeth: to find
The plums all gone, the air dusty, the sun
Facing the other way; to think that here
We do resemble the supposed best owner:
Angry when fruit is innocently stolen.

Silkies

Riding the swell, we watch the seals
still on their rocks.
A yellow one, curved like a grub,
rocks slightly on its chest; another,
brown with big eyes, slithers toward
the water's edge, hesitates
on the broken stone: you sense the fur
of the mammal, the cold skin of the sea.

I love to see them riding nothing,
but I keep still
not to disturb their afternoon
in the chilly glen. They don't look wild:
their odd variety of colour
makes not a family or a herd
but a bored harem, not much good.
They lie there waiting, each alone.

My father grew up across there
(the only house):
he says they kept them off, then.
Seals eat so many pounds of fish;
they kill for fun, more than they need.
A man who lives on fish must
learn to kill seals: he learns the fun
of hitting when they rise to breathe.

Long before that some early man
made friends with seals,
feeding them apples and smoked fish;
stroked them and found their favourite places,
and mated with them, on the sand
or in the deep grass of such isles
as these, too small to farm or walk.
It's said they took him off with them.

I suppose wild creatures for new feelings
could take to man,
prefer him to their casual mates
and swoon with him on land; but quickly

recalled to natural beds of water,
would show him (gasping) how to love
with muscles of their element;
and he for pleasure fail to breathe.

But we go on. My cousin turns
his noisy boat
round to Loch Beag, the waterfall,
back past the house, where the five boys
before the Great War lived their hard,
envied, legendary life.
Like a wet breath the rain falls.
Far off the silkies lie, at home.

V

On the Appian Way
(1984)

This poem represents a journey from Rome to Brindisi, more or less following the Via Appia south to Capua and Benevento, and then branching off left to the Adriatic coast and down again towards the heel of Italy. It is the journey of 365 Roman miles that Horace covered in 37 BC in Maecenas' comfortable travelling-coach, meeting his patron at Terracina on the third evening, and Virgil and two other poets (later to be the first editors of the *Aeneid*) on the fifth day at Sinuessa (by Mondragone), spending the tenth night at a place whose name 'cannot be said in verse', and reaching Brindisi on the fifteenth day.

Horace (then aged twenty-eight) wrote a poem describing the journey and it came out in his first published collection (*Satires*, Rome, 35 BC, poem 5). His poem is a straightforward though amusing 104-line record of the trip. It silently draws on earlier travel-poems, notably one by Lucilius, but it includes (with one exception) no allusions to historical events, however important, that occurred in any of the places passed through or near. The one exception is the remark that Canusium was founded by the Homeric hero Diomedes.

Horace's poem has been translated by Christopher Smart (in his parallel-text edition of Horace) and by William Cowper, among others. There is a handy modern version, with notes and a map, by Niall Rudd in his Penguin Classics volume *The Satires of Horace and Persius*, 1973.

I am indebted to the great Apulian poet (and doubtless also to his Etruscan patron) for giving me an excuse for returning to Italy and the pleasure of writing about it. I am grateful also to Northern Arts for subsidising my journey with a travel-grant.

Newcastle upon Tyne
February 1983

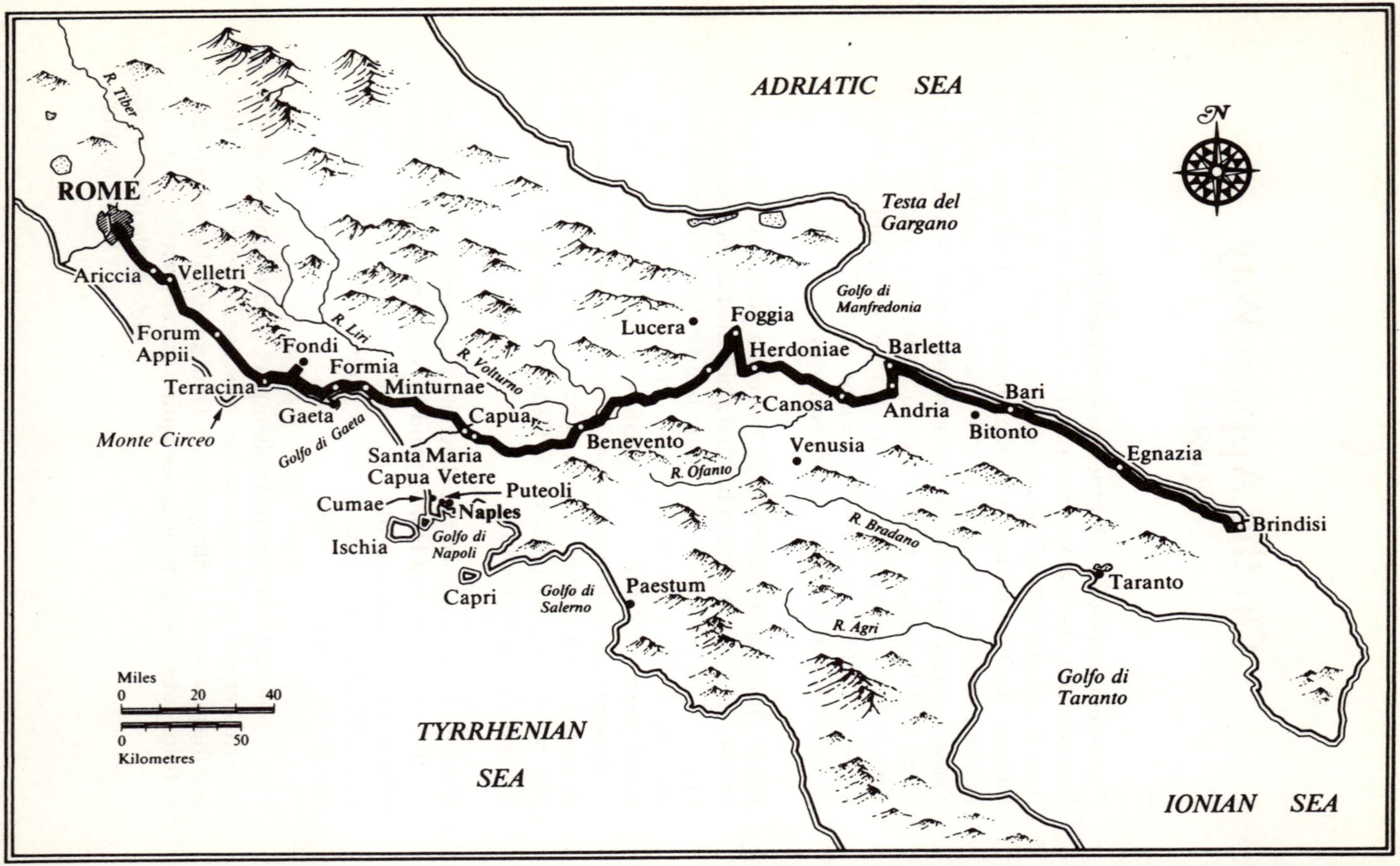
ADRIATIC SEA
ROME
R. Tiber
Ariccia
Velletri
Forum Appii
Terracina
Monte Circeo
Fondi
Formia
Gaeta
Golfo di Gaeta
Minturnae
R. Liri
R. Volturno
Capua
Santa Maria Capua Vetere
Cumae
Puteoli
Naples
Ischia
Golfo di Napoli
Capri
Benevento
Lucera
Foggia
Herdoniae
Canosa
R. Ofanto
Venusia
Testa del Gargano
Golfo di Manfredonia
Barletta
Andria
Bari
Bitonto
Egnazia
Brindisi
R. Bradano
R. Agri
Taranto
Golfo di Taranto
Golfo di Salerno
Paestum
TYRRHENIAN SEA
IONIAN SEA
Miles
0
20
40
0
50
Kilometres

DAY I: Domenica di Pasqua
(April 19, 1981)

"Flying from great Newcastle upon Tyne,
First stop Ariccia on the Alban line
And a pensione with the Christian name
Of Piccolo Paradiso, I became
The single occupant of a marriage bed."

Sounds fun – but that was travel-in-the-head,
Written before I came: my room is sold,
I understand, half hearing what I'm told,
Still deaf with flying – or with coming down.

I catch the next bus to a friendlier town,
Velletri, and a paradise just as good
Off up the hill, "Benito's-in-the-Wood."

DAY II: Lunedì di Pasqua
(April 20, 1981)

A cuckoo comforts the shocked traveller
With its familiar Latin: I can hear
Again, even the tears of Jupiter
Gently falling (the Englishness of spring!)
And the rain stopping (birds begin to sing)...
  I drop my book (already started once)
By Bellow ("handsomest of Americans")
And step out, fresh, to Nemi, with one stop
To buy cured flesh in a Velletri shop.
The man cuts rounds, translucent they're so fine,
And pats them down like patience cards in line
Over the greaseproof paper, where they hold
Till he can roll and hand them to me, scrolled,
A salame cigarette; how matter-of-fact
An art! – to mention it's a lapse in tact.

I weigh up Nemi's woods, beyond its lake,
Dull as old mercury, and turn back and take
My Claudia acqua minerale across
Genzano to where kids play moto-cross
On a small hill, above the Ariccian slope.
They don't like me – a stone bounds – but I hope
By quietly eating olives at their view
I prove a foreign beggar's human too.
To prove I'm really here, I take a picture
Across the blurry valley of Ariccia.
The town once lay down there, but rose to get
Its sights on Rome, and got that silhouette.
That long straight track must be the road, declined
Among allotments, that I came to find...
There's no way down. The viaduct around
Shows me an image dubious and profound:
A small brown field, printed in herringbone
Pattern by someone's tread – as it was sown
This morning, I would guess, but not a sign
Of seed or sowing; just the calm design.

The Ariccia church, with two Bernini bars,
Is good for drinks, but hard to see, for cars:
So many pass, so near the steps, my head
Thickens with Roman holiday-makers' lead.
I'm feeling lonely too, and with alarm
Spot bullet-holes in a statue's bronze left arm.
("Menotti Garibaldi, why shoot you?"
"There's always someone disapproves! 'Et tu!' ")
So, at my road (yes, it's the Appian Way
The time-sucked monuments of Albano say)
I hesitate: the weak inertial will
Insists, "Go down this lane." "And up that hill?"
Instinct responds; and with a southbound bus
Halts my safari through the miscellaneous.
This should be all: being carried home for tea.
But a pro-Briton riding next to me
Sadly makes friends for minutes, pays my fare
Back to Genzano, and directs me where
I can find miles and miles of naked Appia.
Which leaves me nervous, but a little happier.

Strange how our species never seems to know
The local sights – I tramp two hours or so
In vain, to see the start of those next straight
Sixty kilometres; almost too late
Back on the bus-route, turning idly round,
I see this magnified roadskin on the ground,
Dark and lumpy. Legs as long as mine
Should dive immediately down that line
To Terracina. But this poet feels
Bound to the ease of other people's wheels;
Ways can get overgrown; it's much less fuss
To barge across those marshes in a bus.
This road becomes that road, in any case –
It just applies black make-up to its face.

Late, I climb to Benito's in the dark
Under the stars, and the tame wolves of Latium bark
Till the horizon rings. They understand
That map, the real properties of land,
In ways we don't – or they proclaim they do:
In fact, their boundaries are notional too,
However marked, and (when the intruder's passed) they think
They like to smell the various types of stink.

DAY III: Martedì
(April 21, 1981)

Why have you come here?, coldly loneliness
Asks as I lose my English social dress
And grope for a peninsular one. Be resolute,
I tell my beating heart: we'll start again on foot:
Go back to Go.
                    A good transistor blues
Sounds in the Valley of the Latin Muse,
And kicking back a ball to Remus' sons
Where Porta Capena was a goal-mouth once,
I pace from Rome; and wandering in and out
Of little churches, Baedeker-devout,
Look forward to the blessing of good food.

Then, is it greed that spoils my gracious mood?
Something about the three grilled quails is wrong...
Like flattened frogs... the fourth looks on without a song...
Or is it envy of the lovers' faces
Bent on each other in these tourist places?

Catacombs are for happy pilgrims; I
Think my imagination has boiled dry,
But, feeling better as the tombs get poorer,
Walk on, reading the elegies – "Hic soror
Et frater" – listening to the stridor of
Cicadas and the springs of parked cars full of love.
That's why the living Romans come: to mate
Among the dead – so many, and so great.
They line the way until the Roman ring
Road roughly cuts such fellow-travelling.
Beyond the ring (no bridge – you run across)
More loving souls still circle at a loss:
At dusk, a thwarted couple from their car
Calls, "Is the Appia Antica far?"
"Coraggio! Su!" I say; "just over there."
"Thank God! We were beginning to despair."

DAY IV: Mercoledì
(April 22, 1981)

Feeling I'm marking time, I try to write,
Then buy a book I coveted last night –
Calvino – from a communist bookshop! – such a treat
I could dictate it to Benito's as I eat.
What laughter! *Cosmicomiche!* He tells
Those astronomical jokes like no one else.
Meanwhile I'm glad (my ego's not been good)
To see two diners copying my food:
Shy slices from a blushing naval gun
Of mortadella, with some onion-
Tomato-and-potato hash in patties,
Followed by strawberries con limone. That is
A shame when lobsters with freshwater thirst
Are scrambling near me to be eaten first,

But there you are: I can't touch arthropods,
Not now; though it might please the sea-born gods
To have one brought to Terracina and instead
Of me plunged back in the polluted Med.

The panorama of our element
Rolls past the bus like an advertisement
For mountain villages. I long for maps
To name the scars on hazy hills. Perhaps
That slope once grew a famous wine...I know
This house on stilts (the tractor lives below)
Is new and has no history yet, but that
Might be some ancient hero's habitat.
The little thrill of breathing Caesar's breath
Gently diverts me on my way to death.
Meanwhile our poplar cage, our window glass,
Protect us from the experience we pass,
The dust and heat, the exhausted afternoon,
The dead dog (and his owner who will soon
Run from a room where he's still happily
Doing what people do at half-past three),
The reek of the canal, and on the right
A magic mountain almost out of sight.

By this canal, with boats now, but still smelly,
Stood the hotel; my sympathetic belly
Revolved, resolved, revolted. I threw in
Four brown grenades of stunning kaolin
And pasta in brodo, and walked along to see
The coast. Could I step twice in the same sea?
Another sea, I think. Another I,
More cautious ("better keep my transport dry"),
Stands by the unmoved blank that's also twenty
Years older.

On the cliff, "Merlino è innocente,"
I read, and "CXX" and "Napoli
Merda". We have to leave a mark don't we? –
The conspicuous expulsion of a thought.
The cliff was not well-written, so I bought
(From a lady bookseller ironing underclothes)
Montale's works (except his lovely prose).

A war memorial in the biggest square
Names "trucidati dai tedeschi". There?
Exactly opposite San Salvatore?
I read the names and itch to know their story.
Who'd tell me? – in my German coat I look
So German. Later, safely, from a book,
I'll learn what happened: if two armies met,
Landings or partisans . . . and then forget.
Meanwhile, made legible with ancient red,
These names remind the oblivious of their dead
From time to time.

DAY V: Giovedì
(April 23, 1981)

Windy; and I can do
What diarrhetics can't; the sky's turned blue;
The old town sails across it; and the new
Resharpened swifts shower down delirious screams:
This is the Italia of our winter dreams.
(What kind of palms are those?) As I go out,
There is a radiant filmstar-friendly Kraut
Like a tank-captain, with his flattened gel
(Bride to the Junker?), striding off as well.
Rising like nausea, wartime prejudice
Astonishes me: will he bounce like this
After he's seen that monument?

I creep
("Properly", pleads my belly) up the steep
Incline towards the duomo. Cappuccino
And sugary bun (somebody else has vino)
For breakfast, standing, in the Forum Bar.
From a municipal speaker – no, a car –
Pop music fills the slippery travertined
Piazza. Some old mayor's shinned up and signed
The campanile with "S.P.Q.T."
The antique building-blocks, AD/BC,
Tactfully switched (as Rome and Augustus fail)
Onto the smaller medieval scale,

Home-made and clumsy, and a mosaic frieze
Childishly romanesque, put you at ease:
Real Sunday-architecture! "In the porch a
Basin" – not that I saw it – "used to torture
The early Christians," Baedeker says. That's why
Inside the holy water stoups are dry
Perhaps, commemorating. In a tent
Glows something white, mysterious monument
To something. Helplessly inquisitive,
The tourist looks for anyone who might give
The alms of information. There's an old
Woman in black – she could be buttonholed,
When she's stopped reading prayers out. (If a Third
Of God is listening, this must sound absurd.)
A priest crosses the floor. But how do you say
"Buon giorno" to a priest? While I delay
(Signore? Monsignore? *Padre?* No!),
He rolls severely past: I'll never know
If that's a relic or some wrapped-up art...

Chilly in here: before my bowels start
Moving, I move outside. The Temple of Jove
(Beardless) attracts me up – not far above,
But what a long way round. Much heavier than
The flashing reptiles on the path, a man
Creeps on two sweating feet: a courteous crowd
Of flowers recognise him with a nod.
The city is abased. The view extends.
The old road straightens, and the new road bends
Up to the temple platform, and a bar.
Below, a civil chopper (meaning war
To me) scratches the city, a small threat
Made suddenly bigger by an airforce jet
Surfing along the hills in silence. I
Engage a little lizard eye to eye,
Rest in his sense of time, and try to bear
The eye of Helios on my thinning hair.
The sun makes him feel full? He whisks at last
Into the weathered chalk. Two shadows passed,
One of a black man; he was being shown
Theoderic's palazzo, every stone
Part of the Ostrogothic builder's plan.

You cannot contradict the local man
Entertaining a guest, but that's not true.
(And how shall truth prevail, if not through you?)
Still, it was fun, in Zeus's portico
Changing my film, to hear him say – and know
He told a folktale – that "Theoderic
Kept horses here; this was his stable." Sic
Transit gloria caeli, either way.

On the great stage two liceali lay
With waving feet, revising for exams
(Trade-cycles; Latin; edible cryptogams;
Physics; history; mathematics)... They
Concentrate while the world holds out its tray
Of treasures to be memorised. Which palls,
After a while... And by some crumbling walls
That have survived the things they guard, I drop
To sea-level and the Lazio Transport stop.
Some half-formed members of our friendly species
Stand there exchanging manuscripts. Inglisc is
The Thursday homework, with apostrophes
And prepositions: "What's he after? She's
Worth looking at." But they're too shy to speak,
And I've sworn off my language for a week.

I went to Fondi for a lemonade
And a shampoo – two hours: a lightning raid
But leisurely, as the churches were all shut.
Nothing to do but seize the immediate
Italian noon. Except the off-stage cooks,
Everyone walks and talks and rides and looks.
A blonde, in glasses silvered by the light,
High heels, white overalls all but too tight,
And a neat navy jacket, went off down
The Corso Appio Claudio: with a model's frown
She reappeared, again, and yet again.
The cop on duty, vigilant and urbane,
Just stood and smoothed his hair back. The damn-fool
Writer sat grinning. On their way from school
Small girls came by, in matching party-frocks
With sashes, and good boys in primary smocks
And black cravats, like small Bohemians,

And last the secondary prancing ones
Irregularly invaded, sidling by
The broken castle, chatting with one eye
Cocked for opponents and who's touching who,
Whose hair's been rearranged, whose scooter's new,
Changes of interest and confidence –
The sub-plot of the town. To see it once
Means little, but the traveller will compare
This civil comedy in the open air
With one of ours, played in a public void –
With the same title: *Young Bloods Unemployed.*

They have good backdrops too: walls of stone dice
Or ancient jigsaw, movingly precise;
Gigantic ashlar; stucco split with scars
Of earthquake or with acne from forgotten wars.
Strolling outside their cage of custom, I
Am unseen, except to an eccentric eye
Like the old man's who caught me staring at
A wall – nostalgic soldiers stare like that:
"Tedesco?" "No." You can't tame memory –
He won't have had as "good" a war as me.
"Inglese." We exchange congratulations:
"My" nationality, "his" fortifications.
Pondering the theory of foreign-ness
I photograph them, and just catch my bus
Back up the old blind censor's long straight Way
Through ads for eyewash ("with collirio", they say).

A film called "Porno-Nurses in the Army"
Hog-calls across the road, but doesn't charm me.

DAY VI: Venerdì
(April 24, 1981)

That night I dreamed my company and guide
Through all this world of sights sat there beside
My bed: one smile made her so beautiful
I leaned my newly-shaved and sensible

Cheek to her delicate untasted breast
(In a silk shirt), the perfect traveller's rest,
Not reaching it, and leaning more and more,
With sheets and mattress fell on the tiled floor.
Unharmed, contented (falling off the shelf
Renews your friendship with your childhood self)
I killed the light, hoping to dream the rest
(Where was the little sister of that breast?),
Blessing the dangerous inns of Terracina,
But... Wasn't that the face of the drycleaner
Who's got my shirts? And did I wake the guest
Next door? The noisiest country in the West
Made noisier – unless like me he packs
His ears for sleep with "malleable" wax.
(Of course, that doesn't stop the noise *inside*.)

The chestnut candles gutter, and subside;
From puddles Polyphemic bubbles eye
The weather, and pop back; the damp swifts fly
Awkwardly, elbowing through the rain that sifts
All crunchy insects out and leaves the swifts.
I plod to get my shirts: by morning light
Maria's harder, not a monk's delight
But a worn member of the working sex;
The Holy Spirit Bank won't change my cheques;
And Jupiter Pluvius pisses himself in heaven.
Postcards; more showers; elevenses; at eleven
Jupiter takes a drink just long enough
For me to stagger dry with all my stuff
Two hundred metres to the bus-stop.

Hills
Fume as if mountains; human breath distils
To water on the windows; pulling on
More and more veils, the modest view has gone,
After Sperlonga, into galleries
Of rock: enormous Rothko skies and seas
Hung on the right, "Nerone Merda" on
The left. By the Motel Laocoon,
In front of me "Brunella" (says her shirt)
Twists on her seat as if her buttocks hurt;
She pulls the hot shirt off; a tomboy breast

Peeps from the armhole of her (brother's?) vest.
No protest, but the Siren's out of place:
She gets off at Gaeta naval base.

This marble coast of shipwrecks, quaint maybe
To landlubbers, turns round this promontory
Into the soft Gulf of Gaeta, not
Lovely today – Where shall I stay? – A lot
Of horrible black stuff over Naples – Hell,
Where's gourmet Formiae? – And an old hotel? –
I need a cicerone. Three men smile:
"Under the railway bridge"; but half a mile
Uphill is that the citadel? I sweat
At the mere thought of sweat and getting wet.
(My books!) From here to Capua on the train
Takes hours of changes; I embus again,
Embarrassed ("Reader, sorry – it was stormier
Than I could bear, the atmosphere of Formia"?)
And frightened (Shall I reach tonight alive?
How badly will this cross-eyed driver drive?
Why can't a conduttore just conduct?)...

Past rubble mushrooms and an aqueduct
We blare, straight on past Virgil's butcher's-shop
In Scauri, hooting where I'd love to stop,
At the "Postiglione" (square with classical roof –
And a conductor?) surely lightning-proof,
With its own theatre (last of Lazio's),
Then whiffling through the struts of one of those
Meccano bridges, past some buffaloes
Neck-deep in marsh, blinking like goddesses
Taking the Garigliano cure for stress.

Campania: small unmilitary lane
With cactus in the hedge, the bruise of rain
Going down in bursts of sunlight, the road starred
With muddy outbreaks from a farmer's yard,
Where we were checked, by fighting on the road:
Three men arguing, not the lorry-load
Being disputed, block the way. We rise
And stare out through the bus's compound eyes;
The farmer kicks the driver in the arse

Full-force; the big-nosed umpire signals "Pass",
And we advance to Sessa. I suppose
The next place was Cascano, but who knows? –
Aged, noon-struck, vacant, its town-hall propped
Up with great sticks; we slowed, but never stopped,
Withdrawing eastwards in a hungry mood
Across a plain laid out with half-grown food.

They dropped me at the turn for Sparanise:
Catching the next coincidence would be easy –
"It's that way." But my travel-angel made
Me taste the salt of autostop. I stayed
Sweating and anxious for a sunny hour
At the cross-roads, unacknowledged, without power,
Until a nuclear physicist stopped his Fiat:
I had an honest face and he could see it...
The wary traveller, clinging to his books,
Gets in behind. "Nice car. Is it a Lux?",
I might have asked him, but his passenger
Opened her great big eyes and made me look at her,
Chinning the front seat. She's a Siamese, a
Dancer; his firm makes helicopters; Lisa,
Gilt thighboots, knitted tights, knitted bumfreezer;
He comes from Mondragone; red gilt hair;
Row out a mile, the water's clear as air,
And you look down on streets and buildings where
Orazio met Virgilio; "Is it Thai
Dancing?" (with temple finger-meanings); "I
Am Thai" (with priestess-paint about the eye
And little-monkey cheek); there's a cassette...
It's her own music... there... but she can't get
It in; he does it; no, not that, not yet,
Turn over (watch the traffic) no, no, not
That, *that;* one sees her, in her solo spot,
Arching, contracting, pulsing all she's got
In the brown skin, while he records the lot
(Twentieth-century toot-toot).

"A Caserta
Per il week-end". (But how does *he* divert *her*?
With stories of his wife and child in Sweden?
Of his escape – divorce – back into Eden

After ten years? With aircraft plans? Is she
A dancing spy? Too thin to spy on me...)
Where should he drop me? Capua Gate? It's better, he
Insists, but Santa Maria Capua Vetere
Is where I want (Good luck! Goodbye!) to stay.
The close-up mood dissolves. They drive away
To their own centre-stage.

No luxury
Hotel: in fact, it takes ENIT
Lists to persuade a grubby citizen
There's a hotel of any sort. There's one.
The lonely man there's watching *Happy Days:*
The rooms, all twenty-nine, are full. He says.
I wonder if my luggage puts him off. He
Still says the same after a cup of coffee,
And, everyone's getting married: unemployment
Addicts men fatally to mere enjoyment.

So, past the prison battlements (armed guards) –
Centre for earthquake victims – propped façades
And portals, to a bus-stop, where I saw
"GLADIATORI – SUNDAY – STARTS AT FOUR"
(A team of widowers: on earthquake day
Irpinia Gladiatori played away).

In the full sadness of periferia
I found the Hotel Capys: Mamma mia,
At last, a letto matrimoniale, here!
Room without windows – still, what newly-wed
Asks for a view? Just showers, and a bed.
Happily pitching camp, marked in a square
With boots, books, toothbrush, new-washed underwear,
I reconnoitre: ramparts lapped in wheat,
Old park where adolescent couples meet
Spied on by avid friends, old hospital
Collapsing (earthquake damage), piazza-ful
Of Capuans, and a narrow railway line
That joins the other Capua to mine.
(Already this one – now I eat – is home.)

DAY VII: Sabato
(April 25, 1981)

Against the gravity that leads to Rome
I drifted through the morning rain to be at a
Saturday matinée in the amphitheatre;
Closed for restauro, but there was a fair
For agriculture-vultures in the square.
Here like an elegant slave a Lamborghini
Tractor waits to be sold, while contadini
Coerce its scarred and mucky ancestor
From America past; a flailing dinosaur
(*Maia Caterpillar!*) yawns, its yellow maw
Roaring for lunch; the shredded-wheat machines
Opposite look at their nails: they don't know what he means;
With watering mouths men crowd a smörgåsbord
Of hand-tools; with a woman's double sword
A man in chains hacks at a coloured cord;
And, larking in the rain, above it all
On a bike, two boys glide round: serenely tall
Because he's standing on the carrier-rack,
One holds up high over the pedaller's back,
Enlarged, half of a burnt-out citrus fruit:
A parapioggia – or a parachute.

This Capuan apparatus makes me want
Restauro too: an artful restaurant,
Not something vague au naturel. One strolls
Past the weird shops ("Drugs and Colonials")
Towards the Restaurant Faust, asking the way,
Losing one's self – it's Independence Day,
A day for weddings – bonbons at church doors –
Almost run over by a cart and horse –
The Faust's been sold, damn it, and by its wall
Gibbers a brown rat, the traditional
Plat du jour of a siege economy.
The midday-walking citizens pass by
Pausing to mock it on the other side.
What can one do? I bought a map. A guide
Was given, and at Gianni's I was fed
What the Campanians prefer to bread.

But I prefer – almost – to pasta, playing
Family Tree: "If that is Gianni saying
Shrug to the phone, showing it what he means
With both hands, who's the small fat boy who cleans
The glasses with his breath? That's not his mother,
Nervously taking orders; that's no brother –
But he's like Gianni... Ah, here waddles in
The simple flesh, the clients' heroine,
Young, flustered, ignorant, with *his* Irish curls..."
Three Romans, wearing woolly-coats like girls
Over their shoulders, with a virile sprawl
That hints at living off and on the ball,
Take their dark glasses off, collect their gear
In handbags and file out, to reappear,
Bright, in the window, as their car leaves with a leap
Towards some action. I retract and sleep.

At five on the Parade Ground I fall in
With other fathers, some with orange skin
And scholarly Asian bodies, whose round sons
Call, "Babbo, andiamo al Circus," like Italians,
And drag them, wounded by paternity,
To pay. The mothers smile indulgently,
Not minding they look fat with folded arms,
Placid for once, not thinking of lost charms
But power; and hug the levers of creation.

Round the arena of our concentration
These parents stir, remembering other rings
And better days, and softer furnishings.
Their children mix; like one sad man, I fear
The audience is the best performer here.
The circle is so empty; and they've skied
All ropes on which an acrobat might ride.
Under the coarse Keplerian tent it's warm...
But two tall solemn blacks in uniform
Roll a red carpet out, and at a run,
With cartwheels, bounces, bows to everyone,
The circus Wegliams family starts the fun:
Even the smallest (is that bulge a nappy?)
Frowningly does the splits to make us happy.
Her uncle clown drags on two horses: they

Run round; he tries to mount. Whatever way
He jumps, he misses; they run slow or fast
Or halt, and he goes sailing (puzzled) past.
The blacks carry him off. A young man shows
Riders can ride – but everybody knows –
Magnificently – but we hardly watch,
Because his partner claps her milk-white crotch
Onto the other horse with a soft smack,
And bumping on and off its lumpy back
Follows him round, her bottom through its gauze
Finally blushing, to our loud applause.

Then animals, charmed and charming, and at once
Forgotten.

Awkward squad of elephants
Trained by a boy.

A clown I shan't forget,
Who makes the lady ringmaster a bet
About an apple, swiped from her: if he
Can hide it, he can have it; they agree.
Between his legs – she finds it; in his hat –
She finds it. Someone interrupts her at-
tention; her back is turned; he eats it. Now
It's better hidden, but she guesses how –
Winning the bet...I like his losing line:
"You *couldn't* find it there, so it was mine."

Mistakes are moving; we can feel the talents
Of an equilibrist who loses balance:
Sweating behind a blindfold he repeats
His climb (we teeter on our plastic seats)
With plank and roller up a flight of stairs,
Then, adding on a tower of kitchen chairs
To the shifting board, springs to the top and stands
On his forehead, whirling hoops on feet and hands.

Even in the gaping moment something burns
Such details (really) from these clever turns
And memory rejects them, as if sights
Were not experience – till, in silvery tights

And silvery shirt, the lady of the ring
Mounted a rope and clung there glittering,
Opened-out, upside down, an X of light
Spun in the face of universal night,
Not to a circle of the lustful, spun
To harmonise the many with the one
Peacefully spinning.

Later, going out,
I saw her (mother of the young mahout?)
In slacks and jacket, and with much to say
("Thanks, Mrs Williams, super show today" . . . ?),
Said nothing, and half-wished I hadn't seen her . . .
These glaring body-arts! Some "medicina
Estetica" would calm me, maybe; but
The doors of those beauticians were all shut.
Still, there was Capys food and drink to make
My windows of perception more opaque,
And company: two security-system men.

When I emerged, to see the stars again,
The street-lamps came between them and my eyes.

DAY VIII: Domenica
(April 26, 1981)

The Lord's Day is a day for heights: I rise
At the sound of the radio bird, wondering whether
Outside my nuptial cave there's climbing weather,
And drop my change all over the damned floor.
Is this the omen? While I'm grovelling for
The coins, I find a stranger's happiness:
A used pink condom in a pool of mess
Under the genial bed's foot; then, the radio voice
("Sant' Angelo in Formis") names my choice.

Shunting my coins for coffee in her coffer
And throwing signals, the Signora makes an offer:
A single room – but for a single night.
I pat her over-sexed Alsatians (they don't bite,
She's warned me), buy some postcards from her parrot,
And try to walk, not dance, to my new garret.
It's sunny, with a view: a rolling cat
In a ploughed field, a farm-house, heat-haze... That
Must be Tifáta! The cat stops to lick,
And my Olympus, drunk with joy, goes "Hic!"

Pulling my boots on, I'm uneasy, though.
It's hard to mount a thing you don't quite know
The name of. Is it Tífata? The Signora's
Not heard of either; and some Young Explorers
(Scouts), beside the Volturno, are so shocked
At climbing anything, their memory's blocked.
"How high is it?" "Who knows? But that's the way."

I cross a sunken road. The sky's gone grey,
Miserable for a climber trudging round
Old city walls into a dumping-ground.
At first, confused by stench, I only see
A chaos of smashed stuff, in tumuli
Of collapsing iron and paper, but – Gesù! –
People (Hansel und Gretel?) live here too
With their collections, cats, plants, socks on lines,
In houses sculpted from the rubbish-mines
Of no-man's-land. Horrible dogs appear,
Starving or staggering, and come much too near.
– Sling at them with the camera! What an end!,
I'm thinking, when a car comes round the bend,
Dispersing them, a vintage car that mocks
At waste with pre-war fashions in a gleaming box.
As more and more survivors, numbered, pass
To their reunion, I take the grass
Beside the road, relieved, almost saluting.

The sun shines. The air moves. I stride on, booting
Cartridges off the path into the wheat
Among the dancing poppies, for my feet
Tingle in memory of the family dead,
All the irrevocably deep in bed.

A bicycle slowly follows me. I stop
Above the motorway, on the bridge top,
And wait. The slope, his one arm, don't prevent
Him pedalling all the way: "Tira il vent',"
He puffs. Below, the sinners in their cars
Whirl north and south. We watch them through the bars,
While he draws breath. Could he have fought? . . . We scan
Each other's eyes and skin, the veteran
Of "Ababa" and Tobruk, the child whose fate
Was Florida. He asks, and I relate:
"I was a boy – the war was not quite real.
I heard of your great battles, which are still
Like legends to me, but" (the empty sleeve)
"One learns . . . One learns . . . The pain . . ." "I didn't leave
My arm in Africa, but here, torn clean
Off by an agricultural machine."
One learns indeed. The wind on such a height
Makes your eyes water . . . Hard, I think, to fight
For home, being wrong. How can I understand?
I shake him clumsily by the left hand,
And he rides on, but slower than he came.

Bar at the cross-roads. "Limon-soda." Same
Question about Tifata, same blank looks.
(When names are dead, they bury them in books?)
I spend my change on Saturn – pinball game
(There's a god honoured still with local fame)
And walk to see the frescoes.

Looking through
The keyhole (other tourists form a queue)
Is all my joy – Sant' Angelo is SHUT
FOR RESTORATIONS; Mass is in a hut
Opposite, full of semi-precious flowers
And sunbursts to repel these April showers.
One notices the tact: we celebrate
Doubting Domaso; women communicate,
Men look away; the rising disk of bread
Is countered by a patter overhead
But no one turns; and when the supper's over
The cup and dish are smoothly wiped. We cover
The sour notes of collection with sweet song

(For nobody gives paper), so among
Dolphins and telephone tokens I donate
The metals left from Saturn to Christ's plate.

A goat-boy puts me on the path – there is
A right way up the crumbling terraces.
The olive-trees are someone's. The hill yields
(Sporadic shots!) a stack of little fields
To someone. It starts raining. A frog speaks
("Brek!") like a native to invading Greeks
And makes me jump. A barely human track
Snakes (till a paw of bramble breaks its back)
Round to the ridge, where someone stoops and picks
Fistfuls of ("Spallicce! Buono!") thin dark sticks.
Wild asparagus? Booming through our silence
Come more explosions. It's the urban violence
Of "Festa" (as he says, and stoops again),
Firing away in the hills across the plain.

On a flat shoulder a wrecked building stands
Among concrete graves or bedstones and commands
Dull vistas of crossbedded sun and rain.
A Scottish shepherd's grandson can't complain
Of this Italian weather...

Those goats bell
And bleat, advancing up in parallel.
A billy (on two legs with trembling knees)
Mumbles the green lobes of the younger trees.
Some of the goats look pink, like fat whippets with ears
Like Bedlingtons. The goat-boy reappears,
Carrying something long which, without warning,
He turns into a hemisphere in mourning,
And bends for spallicce, and whistles to
His flock; I sing across, as goat-men do,
Grazie (for directions), Grazie
(For trespassing on your hill) and Grazie
(For grace – good measure – "thank-you for today").

My heart thumps, thumps. Have other older men
Climbed here, thinking, like me, to come again
One evening, slowly, with a bag, to see

The sun open the world, with company?
Someone's still shooting. Are there gamebirds here,
Or even birds? What's that strange noise? You fear,
In lonely places far too near the skies,
Some brigand hero will materialise
Waving his ancient weapon, and demand
Your traveller's cheques, signed with a shaking hand,
And then the hand; or that some final slope
Will hold you, cragfast, till you give up hope.

Going on all fours up the vertebrae
Of hills wears your warm adult self away
And leaves you bare, too young to be alone
So far from bed and face to face with stone.
Thoughtless above the maybe fatal scree,
You clamp your bony hands to slippery
Clumps of uneaten grass. Behind, below,
Is dank air and the feel of someone you don't know
Watching as squalls approach. Are these your last
Moments of life? You've never crawled so fast.
But here's the chapel; and the rain has passed.

A sad mess: there's an apse, some lipstick-traces
Of fresco (blessing hands and rubble faces),
Three walls against the cloudy centuries.

The last few feet. A grove of flagellant trees
Noisily lashed the east flank of the hill.
The rain abolished height; but, terrified still,
I clutched the rusty twisted summit-rod.
Food cheers me up: I threw the hungry god
(If any) half my rotten African fruit.
Surprised, Jove held his water. I could shoot
Vesuvius, triangular and new,
And crumbling Cumae – westwards, pointed to
By straight roads. But the rules of men down there
Aren't binding on the aimless spirits of air;
The top felt dangerous: "Go. You can't survey
That villa just across the airy way,
Or this side of that egg-cup amphitheatre."
Was there a goddess in the grove? I had a pee at her,
And slid back to the chapel, dining room

Of thrushes (fat brown snails), and crossed the fume
Of someone's Sunday dinner (from a farm
In the dead ground under the mountain's arm),
Down to the pylon line – again you meet
That scent: the hill itself smells good to eat –
Monte Origano! bush the pounding breeze
Spices the pastures with... A crowd of trees,
Wildly occupying their ruin, waves
Me past its nameless non-committal graves
To oversee the Capua road. A blade
Of wet horizon flashes, like a cannonade.
A bus traverses, drawling its two notes.

In a ravine the owner of the goats
Ambushes me for conversation. He
Makes a career of curiosity
As Capo Polizia, goats and sheep
Being relaxation (from the company he has to keep?).
But... "sheep"! The shepherd's grandson eyes a shorn
Pink "Bedlington", and it stares back with scorn.

He once had more – he hesitates – with my eyes
I say, "No hurry", and, "I sympathise."
Well, his nipotu asked for help to get a
Job in the north. He gave this nephew "sette
Milioni" for travel, lodging, food and (glance)
Drink; but the youth made nothing of his chance
And came home penniless: all he'd done (it seems)
Was spend the substance of his uncle's dreams;
And later ask for more, another try:
"E no!" He looks for disagreement in the sky,
Sensing that I agree, but even so
Shy of the naked, sensible, selfish No –
He'll give the confidence to my foreign ear,
But not to eyes, which look, and look severe.
And then the goat-boy comes, the son, the heir
Of herds, and schoolboy who, I see, takes care
Of Babbo's pets on Sunday. "Grazie"
(For being there – and showing me the way) –
My hands are still too clean for him to shake –
"Addio."

Past houses damaged by the quake,
Held in the village wash-house by a shower,
Led on by thirst, deflected by the power
Of laughing schoolgirls, I approach again
The bus-route and the cities of the plain.

At the cross-roads it occurs to me: where they sell
Earth-juice, earth-pictures may be sold as well.
The pump-attendant: "Ask Don Somebody
There by the gate" – the fascist personality
In old age, maybe: a coiffure of white
Horses plunging in rows; brown; lean; upright;
Testy (a carless vagabond should enjoy
His virgin evening!). "Maps?" He sends his boy,
Who fails to find them, and is sent back, trying
To cope and not be seen by anyone crying,
While I, pacific fool, narrate the ascent...
"Of San Nicola?" (with astonishment)
"On such a day?" "Eh! But I'm here today."
"So are you German?" "No. Scozzese." "Eh!"
He'd lots of English friends, from '44,
"Major Brodest, you know him?" and two more
Who played the piano and harmonica (*kiss*)
The best he's heard, and lady officers, Miss
Roma, Miss Mary. After lunch they'd come
From town on horseback, and he'd ride with them
Around the country. Once he'd raced the major
To church ("from my palazzo") for a wager
In wine. "Brodest" had won the wine, of course –
He'd *erba medica* to feed his horse.

"*Medica?* Persian grass? Or, *medical?*"
"No: it *comes from America* – they just call
It *erba medica* here – excellent food
For horses – mine had nothing half as good
In those hard times." He still feels gratitude
Towards his British officers – they got him
Exonerated. (Others would have shot him?)
"I was in the Twenty-Five" – as one might name
A doubtful battle, with both pride and shame,
That he had fought, avoiding the long arm
Of history, keeping the family farm.

"I am against," he adds. Against the time,
The people, anything. "Did you ever climb
That hill? – Tifata, isn't it?" "To us
It was the chapel of Saint Nicholas."
The bus is coming as I turn to see
The hill through its new name; delightedly
The boy comes running with two maps; de haut
En bas, the don presents them; and I note,
Glowing on the bus steps, the maps are free –
Omaggio – given, by that feudal man, to me.

The Capys doormat, like a baby's grave
On the threshold, choked with dust, says, "Hello SLAVE" –
No, "SALVE" – to my boots. They've had their day
Supporting my scarred shins, and can be put away.
Then down to eat bistecca please, not VEALS,
And talk about the Campanian ways and meals
With the two other guests, both Torinesi
Who think all southerners are soft and lazy.
Their smiling Alpine (almost Austrian)
Accents assert there's work for everyone
Who looks. Of course, their work would make them hard:
Their sicurezza that can guard a guard.
We drink to Italy – we should drink to Hell:
Satan makes work for honest hands as well.
Then, once around the block, to ease the rigour
Of too much life, and to control my figure,
Grinning and rolling in my wealth of sleep.

DAY IX: Lunedì
(April 27, 1981)

A tap of sunlight on my lids: they creep
Up like the orb itself, the rudely measuring sun
Behind Tifata (1981
Feet, says my Admiralty handbook). "Ssss,"
Breathes someone's beard to an electric kiss...
No, as I take the wax out of my head,
It's sparrows at their orisons; the bed-

Side clock ("Five Rams" from China) – no, that's dead;
A buzzing from across my field – the station.

There's no one there to deal me information
Or tickets. In a waiting-room I meet
Two evil eyes: cornered, hunched on her seat
Like a black owl in rags, she shrieks at me,
"Ma che biglietto? Non viaggiare oggi!
Cattiva fortuna!" *Captain Reason* leaves,
Running, as hurt as someone who believes.

Not having travelled on an animal,
I don't know if it's wheels themselves that lull
The tactless passenger, just sitting there
While landscape's borne (for judgement) past his chair;
But, after yesterday, I miss the feel
Of covering ground, and weaken on this steel.
Rubber's better: buses won't let you skirt a
Place-name demurely; you must penetrate Caserta
Through the back streets and burst into her square
And let your nose recover in her air.
However, like a city on a tray
Lofted by a divine garçon, it's whirled away,
Royal barracks and all, the pale spring haze
As flattering to it as a candle's rays.

Our carriage up the single track's pulled through
The rifled mountain-side, still smoky blue
From being fired, into the sun, to perch
Above hand-printed houses and a home-baked church
With coloured icing: Maddaloni? There
Like a confession on the public air,
I overhear a woman in the corner
Telling her fellow-workers, "Non son buona."
No one was shocked but me. They all kept calmly sitting
And I heard clicks: she wasn't good at knitting!

Tousled and fresh, spring wakes the upland farms.
A small stream, aching for the sky-god's arms,
Arches and bucks and wriggles in its bed.
I watch it, anxious for the watershed
Of Italy, as if there were just one,
Misreading splashes like a Saracen.

It's the same valley though, when two young heroes strap back on their epic yellow gear
And step out loaded. (I'd have asked them why –
To climb some innocent mountain? or to try
To find lost bits of archaeology? – but
I'd sworn to keep my English word-hoard shut.)

The train squawks; someone in a new red hat
Waves us on with a little round green bat.

Villas hold forth on knolls: obedient vines
Join hands and grow attentively in lines;
A right old olive keeps them straight, as in
The habit of a former discipline;
The hills sharpen, like chunks of layer-cake
Flung at an enemy giant (it's earthquake
Country, this honeymooners' habitat);
A greying haystack, comfy as a cat,
Rests on its elbows, safer than a villa
On slopes where home itself becomes the killer;
And there's a broken bridge.

This gallery
Of nature's happy pictures tires me
As much as works of art. Besides, the seer
Resents the wooden rails that numb his rear.
To Benevento, straight!

– where I regain the street
Pleased as a lover back on his two feet
In sunny circulation. But I stand
Too long, too empty, with too much unplanned:
Bed, transport, food – decisions oscillate
Like swords over my appetite for fate.
Dear Shanks's pony, get us out of this
Quick, before angst becomes paralysis:
We gallop up the street into the first
Hotel, the "best" so far (the room's the worst –
Undusted since the earthquake) and make good
The ghost's defences with both wine and blood.

At the next table the grey-haired seigneur's
Reflecting on his rights, and she on hers:

Old, but the only woman in the room,
She tastes lunch faintly through connubial gloom.
Calvino's story (propped against my plate)
Is about love: in the primeval state
Before the big bang, all his characters
Cohabit in the one-point universe –
No wonder now, commercial travellers
In plastic or biographers of Space,
They long for our return to that good place
Where everything was, and the beloved face.

But I'm distracted by a working lunch
In the far corner, where two top-dogs crunch
A contract over: their lieutenants wait,
Foodless around the food, to hear their fate.
They're arguing; something's gone awry; the boss
Is angry; others, loyally, are cross
Or quiet; huge young men, executives,
Arrive, explain, are censured; the boss gives
A side-dish and some cheese and fruit to one,
Who's solved the problem. Wondering what he's done,
I guess I wouldn't learn if I enquire:
I call the shabby waiter, and retire.

Old towns rise to a centre: up then, for a
Spit in the bony bed of the Calore;
Right, for a children's game under a statue
Of Apis; left, to have a stone thrown at you
(Or popped heavily from the powdered yellow
Cheek of the wall) with vengeful cries of "Hello"
And traffic, snarling that an ill wind blew
You here to suffer as the citizens do;
Near where some Roman baths were excavated
By a bomb in '43 (the guidebooks date it
But coyly don't say whose it was) I dodge
Past lonely smiles of welcome from the lodge
Into the theatre.

                                        Three young girls play catch,
Singing a version of a foreign snatch
Till I appear: "Your audience has come –
Don't stop," I say, but only strike them dumb.

My own tongue's twisted; I become a stammerer
Salty with sweat, ashamed, holding my camera
To hide some nakedness. How do I claim
Myself, they ask; my fatherland; and why I came.
I name my island and confess my name
Is Greek, and speak it the Italian way;
"I'm here to visit an old friend," I say,
Rather than seem a tourist; "Who are you?"
"I em Maria. Dis is Anna" (who
Seems to be simple). "Grazia." – Full of grace,
I think, the brown eyes in the Samnite face,
Which nods to where the Roman lions roared
For Christians. "No!" – the bloody traveller's bored –
"This is for plays, not games: the Word and not the Sword . . ."
But they were born here, can't believe they're wrong.

I leave the darkening theatre to their song,
Swoopingly sad: did I come here to see
The stones and hear the ghosts of Italy?
The only nymphs I've met! I should have caught
Them in my camera! Why else was it bought?
Who cares how badly their tradition's taught?
These leaden feelings are disgraceful – old
As all of them together, less controlled!
And can Sofia – not the Puteolana –
Santa Sofia – give me back mens sana?
Yes: in the honey-grove of marble boles
A priest's inspiring some dejected souls,
Who all look up; with different kinds of awe
We see ten arms of stone bend down and touch the floor:
The resolution we were asking for.

I count my money and decide to eat
At the Trajana (tables in the street),
But there the waiter's ill – the ageing cook
Must take the orders, cook, serve, keep the book –
So I walk on, feeling the town's not well,
Through Middle-Eastern gloom, to my hotel,
And wondering who's in power here, to have banned
Escape by bus – except to Sirenland.

Day X: Martedì
(April 28, 1981)

Somebody's poisoned all the air-wells. Oh,
It's five. But that's all right: somehow I know
My angel's back: in the dark, the gutters flow.
At seven there's the antiquated wash
With a hotel hand-towel and the modern Boche
Pleasure of shaving dry in bed. My mind's
In order and enjoys the world it finds.

The money-shops are strange, though: I can boast
Of being denied twice by the Holy Ghost;
The Bank of Naples also tries my mood
By offering such poor rates I'm nearly rude;
The Bank of Samnium's packed with very old
Peasants (fed up with sleeping on their gold?);
The Cassa di Lavoro, a huge oil
Painting of oblongs in five shades of soil,
Poses its clients, all with portrait-faces,
In adoration round two counter-places;
The Italian National Tourist Entity
Has no cash in the safe – or else no key;
Time's wasting, so I go back where I'm sent – to
The Neapolitan Lords of Benevento.

To calm myself ("Dear Money, You're terrific!")
I stop and read an obelisk in hieroglyphic
(And Greek) addressed to "Queen of Heaven, Divine
Mother", and as I trace the bottom line,
Find myself bowing low at Isis' shrine.
Some monumental well-bred couples leaning
On elbows in the Duomo wall look down with meaning
(They've not been served for ages), as I eat
In the Rosticceria Duomo, on my feet –
Not frightening little saucy carcasses –
Something less obviously what it is,
Part of a foreign food-chain – bits and pieces
Discreetly swathed in green stuff changing species.

The train's late; we can talk. A lovely tall
Old woman, brown and lined, not shy at all,

Looks at my bags: her grand-niece speaks for her:
"Sir – are you a committed traveller?"
"Well, sort of, but I. . ." "Do you represent
Boots?" "What? No, it's just more convenient
To tie them on the case like that." For fear that they
Ask where I'm going – not a name to say
To ladies – I inquire their destination.
They're bound for Greci – That's the double station
With Savignano – Have I heard of Tre
Fontane? Lots of tourists come their way
To photogaph; but what, they cannot say.
Possibly them, I think – and later look
In vain for their paese in a book:
Two fly-specks on a map, maybe the very
Reason and heart of some itinerary.
I shake my head. Smiling, they challenge me
To follow when they speak as en famille.
It's not a dialect; it's Albanian
(Greci!). In the paese everyone
Speaks it, but nobody can read it. She's
Gathering patriotic literacies
For them at Naples: soon they'll see the word
In print that up to now they've only heard.

The train arrives: I blunder through all comers
To a compartment full of student plumbers,
And smoothly Benevento leaves, before
I can enjoy it from my carriage door.
But, the spring air at little stations! We
Lean out to platform-flowers at Paduli.
We follow a new stream – not much of one,
You'd think, just up to glittering in the sun,
A mountain-sculptor though, as shall be seen
Beyond this skyline, at its first ravine,
After Corsano. One of the plumber-boys
Explains his friend, who makes so much rude noise,
Is sordo-muto spastico – "Peccato!" – I'd
Assumed he suffered from the sin of pride
Being so handsome, not a carnal flaw. . .

The unknown ranges on tip-toe endure
The metal worm, shuddering as we drill

Clean through the socket of another hill
And reach a halt. Far up, white towns impend:
"Greci? Addio!" (My Albanian friend.)

Now we accelerate: the water's flowing
Downhill with us; somehow you feel you're going
Homewards, with gravity. The mountain-knees
Draw in their skirts abruptly here, and ease
Us out of smoking rock onto the rich
Playing-fields of Apulia: the Chess Pitch.

My ticket-readers say, "Qui scendere"; I get down
Looking unhappily for the invisible town.
I'm nowhere; I should get back on the train.
A railway man points to the windy plain:
A bus will come. Oh good, a bus again.
A sunny day, I tell the buried players
Of chess, and listen to the peaceful airs
In their young wheat, Ceres encouraging
The field and me; and for a while I sing
In harmony with the local wind: that's how it feels
Repeating here the songs I sing to Scottish seals.
A tourist bus comes up and snorts at me,
Stopping as if from curiosity –
"Where are you going?" "To the Golden Dawn" –
But when I seem quite harmless I'm hauled on
Inside among grim darkened faces, men in coarse
Uniform cloth – the working town's whole force.
The toil of travel must seem light and phony
To one who blunges clay and bakes mattoni
For life; the man beside me's too well-bred to show it,
And I politely hide the name of poet.
The company sings – until the driver calls
For silence where he turns toward the walls.

The Alba d'Oro's brand-new. As if I
Have come to stay a fortnight – or to buy
The stunning green mobile of winter wheat
That fills the enormous window where you eat,
The albergatrice, young and very loud,
Shows me all round, embarrassingly proud,
Plump as a good cook... and I'm in her power,

With a dear double room. I take a shower,
Pleased with the view over my drying underwear: a
City in convoy, steaming west – Lucera?

Somebody's ripped the town-walls off. No gate;
You just walk in. Three small boys supplicate
For ice-cream money by a house with shells
On the front, but I'm held back by nothing else.
Even the chill – the sun will soon be gone
("Another teatime missed") – propels me on
Along the Via Ecana, away from posters (*A
Qualcuno Piace il Caldo* at the cinema!),
Into the Duomo. Churches are designed
For morning though, the daily birth of mind,
Our modest resurrections. I must see
The carving on that ambo properly,
And preferably hear a priest compete
With the lion eating the lamb around his feet.
But now, postcards will do.

The bookshop chap
's from Rome and seems a scholar. What mishap
Brought him to sell Third-World theology
In this benighted vineyard? But for me
(Finding some folk-tales on the Gramsci shelf
And, since a poet educates himself,
A paperback of Political Culture styled
Aretine's Postures), he'd have given a child
Some sweets and sold a razor to a woman –
That's all. Strange setting for a learned Roman...
A literary city without peer
Of course, but who is even literate here?

The sun leaves a green sky. Across the street,
"Signore!" – the brickman from the next bus seat
Invites me to his club. I say, "But I'm
Expected back – perhaps another time –
Your Duomo's beautiful." He shows me to
An older church. We both say "voi" for "you".
Two friends of his appear, eager to get
Their card-game started and to have a wet:
They tilt imaginary glasses. I

Repeat my vague excuse for staying dry.
"Is your wife with you?" (They're my age.) I say,
"I'm here alone." "How did you get away?",
They wonder, smiling. "Well, I came to see
What Horace saw, from Rome to Brindisi."
This makes them roar with laughter: "Furbo, eh!"
Three handshakes, bows, and they go off to play,
Leaving the poet hard at work, touché.

Fat arms akimbo (want a fight?), her voice
Suddenly brazen, she proclaims the choice:
A noble sole (far from the sea) or flesh
(That calf's-ear thing with juice, perhaps not fresh).
"Please, I'd like something... new to me, but old
To you... a recipe too secret to be told..."
(Dare I say "local" or – she's looking bored –
"A dish you'd long for if you died abroad"?)
Upstairs I've got a book that fills my mouth
With water – *Tastes of the Italian south.*
My mind's full of its pictures, but one word
Comes out, "Salsiccie?", which she makes absurd:
"Sausages! If you like." Her little daughter,
Sulky (oh, they've been fighting), sooner than she ought to,
Bangs down the half-cooked bangers; I'm still pack-
ing pasta down and make her take them back,
Unfrozen in hot water and parboiled –
Great, if you must feel how your guts are coiled.
A Scot can stomach that; what does alarm us
Is finding under the pillow strange pyjamas.
I bolt the door – and sleep, until at five
Apulia wakes, and starts to look alive.

DAY XI: Mercoledì
(April 29, 1981)

Bags, boots, books, laundry and myself I sling
Into the seat the landlord's offering
To help me get away: his wife's upset
And puzzled (have I seen the Duomo yet?),

But makes the bill up, wondering why I hate
Those road-drills quite so much (they alienate
My wits from me); she loves the way the things vibrate.
She's noisy too, though. Maybe deaf. Is he?
Not that I notice. Though he's easily
Old enough to have fathered her – and me,
Almost, the pig in the middle of our ages.

He works in Foggia, selling pilgrimages:
Sant' Iago, Lourdess, Pa Rhys, and Lon Donne.
Pilgrims to London? "Many were undone
And now are saints. Your Queen Elizabeth..."
Enriched her land with venerable death
(I think). His leaflet doesn't name the sites
They'll bow or kneel at; only, LONDRA, for two nights.
"You live there?" "Further north, near Hadrian's Wall."
"Sant' Adriano?" "No, the imperial
Adrian" – who had the little breastwork built
To keep our noble savage in the kilt
Out of the garden of England.

Monuments
To the immenser dead who lived here once
Slump by the verge. This road is an antique,
I stumblingly guess. Has it a name in Greek?
"Asfalto? If you like old roads, the best
Round here is Hannibal's. By the main way west
They've left a bit exposed..." No telling him
In England roads like this were made by Grim
Or even the Devil, not our ancestors...

Ecco Foggia – the hour when families disperse
For work; "Thanks for the lift"; he sets me down
And I contend through bodies across town
To a park-bench where I write cards, and drink
Saint Pilgrim's orangeade, and watch the shadows shrink,
Like other marginals who here, off-stage
And unemployed, have time to feel their age.
Under their eyes, I quell the anxious dreams
Of travel, and set out the humbler themes:

"My feet still hold me up"

"Half round the course"
"Yesterday had to go by iron horse,
Bussing today"
"Quite fit, from carrying more weight
Progressively – new books, not something that I ate
(In fact, I'd not write home about the food)"

"Your razor's useful. I tap out the chewed-
Up bits of me as offerings to the god of loos.
It seems to work – my stomach's kept the truce"

And – this is clownish, but it's really felt –

"Thanks for the home-made towelling money-belt."

It's comforting – it's the right scale for us –
To skim the dirty earth in a clean bus,
Vroom, vroom. I almost spoil this ancient joy
By getting out my new Olympian toy –
I'd like a picture, down the bus, of this long straight...
But without lorries... or that breakdown... Wait
Till we get past this jogger – on his own, here?
He must be from that new Hotel Herdonia...
Look! a dust-devil dancing among vines
For lack of water, or for stronger wines...
Now it's Cerignola, with balconies
And a street-market, that directs my eyes
Out of the view-finder – and into views.
I pack my traps away, content to cruise.

We stop – a field – nowhere – a filius terrae,
Carrying a bag of tools, appears. We stare. I
Ask where he's going, half imagining
He's an earth-doctor seeing to the spring.
He's going home, thirty kilometers; he's
A contract-journeyman: he prunes olive trees.

We roll – a bishop's move – south-east. The road
Crosses a river flattened like a toad
And nearly dried, with an Islamic bridge
Pinning it to the ground, and tilts us to the ridge,
Past an old arch triumphant over greenery,

To where Canosa's walls keep out the scenery.
We piston quickly down the Corso.

Look,
There's an albergo, listed in the book –
He should have put me down before – Oh hell,
Miles to sweat back – He promised a hotel.
What? Just across the pavement? Here? But there's
No sign! Just through that wicket and upstairs?
Courtyard – Four flights of marble – Dark old door
Saying "Boemondo", open – Hall and corridor
Serenely cool, and empty – Time to see
A room with tables and white napery
(The best sort of environmental art)
And (kitsch as cosy to a Scottish heart)
The Monarch of the Mist, His Mountain Home –
Stags ("after Taylor Adams") in the gloom
By a De Chirico and a Piranesi.
What better omen, when you're feeling lazy,
Than this: a countryman came here – to feast
On the rich menus of the Middle East?

Then, crasc! some glass breaks in Italian.
The selfless spirit of an eldest son
Drives me out on the landing. Back from shopping,
A whitehaired lady watches liquor dropping
Over the lips of steps: "Just vinegar;
Lucky." I pick the food up, then help her.
She's the Signora – the Albergo's full,
Weddings, you know – but wait, it's possible –
She shifts a best man in beside a groom
And gives me the most memorable room:
Broad, low, not squared off, airy, high up, old
Like a white cave with plumbing (both taps cold)
And beds (with patchwork) where the tired can hide
And hear the swifts suggesting joy outside.

Talk begins between tables: if you sit
Receiving Their reflections, You become an It;
Grooming Them back, you find humanity.
By cheese-and-fruit I've joined a coach and three
Heroes from the Canosa football team –

They play on Sundays, so I'll never see them –
And they can't see the bait I cast to fame,
But somehow we're companions in the game.
The coach, tall, calm, waved hair a Celtic pink,
Asks, "Are you a professional bard?" "I think…"
"And if you are, what's a professional?" "Er…"
"Wouldn't you say, more than the amateur,
He loves his work – and is rewarded more
By quiet fidelity than a solo score?"
"Certainly; but…" "So, as we've said, he should
Pour all his energy into getting good?"
Paolo, opposite me, with rich dark curls,
Knows this means him – his goals are often girls –
And cites that happily post-coital chap
Who won the gold (that runner in the cap
At the Olympics), then: "The real professional,
To you, must be a talented obsessional…"
"Eh! No!" And yet I notice the distraction
This coach condemns is simply sexual action –
What the mind does is nothing – Enzo's free
To read, in his spare time, for a degree.
I leave the dialogue – words to them are cheap,
But poets give up life for beauty-sleep.

Here (for once) they have water in the stoup,
Though not that clean, and in the holy soup
A small stone fish hovers, a friendly thing
Moved by our unsuccessful guddling.
The poaching traveller has to feel for One
Pleased with this toy and with his natural Son –
But I pass by where two Lucanian cows
Support the best seat in the bishop's house,
And sit alone in BOAMUNDUS' tomb,
Best resting-place for miles (except my room).
He earned it: born to rule the south, at four
Declared a bastard; self-made prince of war;
Captured and died crusading for the Fish:
His mother brought him here for his last wish.

Smiling, still sleepy, people dawdle through
The piazza as I think what next to do.
A travel-film, *Viaggio nell' Orgasmo,*'s on –

Some tributary of the Amazon –
But I go home, and drink the evening air
With the Signora, on a kitchen chair
At a French window, watching in the square
Late tourists cut the stream of citizens,
And talking family; for we both have sons,
Shouldering now through a flood-tide of men.
Sometimes the lost ones look at you again
Through other faces; though the face is hers,
Another widow's, not my grandmother's,
Feelings pass in the words as if some chance
Remained of touching the neglected hands,
As if a blind old woman long since dead
Could send me comfort and be comforted.
Here the imaginary grandson blurts
Out that he needs some help with dirty shirts;
It's the exterior that you can't keep clean.
She says, "There's that poor girl you might have seen,
Who's been too ill to work, and quite alone
Since that extraordinary bosom's grown –
She'll do them." And she does them, with a smile
Out of a world of growth where nothing's vile.

We watch the news – the faces that this week
Swim to the surface of the box and speak –
And Paolo (he's the curly-head) asks how
It is my troops (we give each other Thou)
Occupy Northern Anger – how we blame
The Russians, who have only done the same –
We should get out, with our expatriates,
And leave it to the Anger democrats.
Less fluent, with less facts, less sure I'm right,
I defend liberty against free fight,
The elector against self-appointed bosses
And everyone from ideologues with crosses.
"There were injustices; but, Paolo, you
Ask for the rule of many by the few."
He's almost speechless, but then talks so fast
(It turns out he plays wing) the bard's outclassed.
Raging, he says it twice: "History must
Now be unravelled, to make Ireland just.
You should repatriate the bloody Prots

To England – or to Scotland if they're Scots."
"But earlier still, the Scots *are* Irish; they
Should be repats in Ireland. Anyway,
They're Irish now, everyone's interbred,
We can't all sleep in Eve's and Adam's bed.
Of course, the Anglo-Saxon part of me
Comes from some wood in what's now Germany.
I'd hate that. (Would the wood be there?) And you?
Where do you think you'd be deported to?"
He sulks. I like him. Rightly he's depressed
His colleagues take the arguments of a guest.
He's violent too. I ask them all to note
My government is mine, not from my vote,
But a majority on one day's poll:
To which I must assent, and not just thole.
So, I say, peace: a thing we fight to keep;
And leave the fight, and take the gift of sleep.

DAY XII: Giovedì
(April 30, 1981)

Breakfast is best, even for Britons, in a bar:
There a gold doughnut, glistering like a star
With sugar, bathes in western coffee. Yours
Makes you a lion wiping frothy jaws
As you prowl off up Hector Proudfly Street.
A
Diagonal of steps leads up: Salita
Arco Diomede; but no arch, they say,
Recalls our founder who in one mad day
At Troy revenged us on the worst goddess,
Tearing her hand and her ambrosial dress,
And the worst god, who balances in red
The excessive profit she contrives in bed.

Above his citadel the swifts design
(In terms my camera's eye can not define)
Their armillary spheres of territory.
Staring through haze towards Mount Vulture,

I hide my compass – with a map like this
I feel a spy on their acropolis
(The swifts', the flowers', the bees'). I wish my dear
Old Yorkshire friend with the sharp eyes were here:
He'd find a Swabian coin, arrowheads, shards,
Astragals, rhytons smashed by Norman bards...
But me – a pair of turning butterflies,
Clockwise and anticlockwise, mesmerise.

You can't see distances – Apulia's dew
Hanging protective tissue on the view –
Only the Appia, vanishing toward
Fields of engraved perspective: the Chess Board.
Some foreground lumps (decaying chess-men?) give
The bland expanse a pinch of narrative.
South, there's more haze: hills of old porridge puff
Dust in the air, a barely paler buff,
Getting it hot. Hung over, today's man
Pores on Canosa's town- (or battle-) plan:
Roads lancing in; the first streets in a ring
Attacked by grids; reluctant contouring;
Fans of orientation; piazzas thrust
In anywhere noble houses bit the dust.
It looks quite senseless now. Meandering down
You'd soon get lost in this disjointed town
If not for pumps, with people, stuck at joints –
They can't speak *lingua*, but the dumbest points.

Upstairs in the Museo, I half fall
Asleep (the Muses' bedroom, after all)
Over a case of weapons, and half waken
("Is war a bore?") on being overtaken
By the Curator and an officer. (Braid
And leather trim a dark-blue tailor-made...
Carabiniere.) This young man has power,
The older hopes, to guard his Muses' bower,
Their little perfume-tubes and breastplates, pins
And swords, and bright green mirrors. He begins
Praising the ancients for their cleverness:
"...Thumb there. That one's for women. Obvious,
When you've been shown." I eavesdrop too discreetly
And miss these things that suit one sex so neatly –

Statues? Cups? He continues with his fears:
Pirates will steal his ancient bright ideas.
"We need a sentry." It would be a crime
To lose again the treasures rescued once from Time.
The policeman's most polite – "But really" –
In fact, the visit is pure courtesy.
So much needs guarding... Helmetless, I run
My brains to safety through the lunchtime sun.

Insects revive the first – when softer light
Commands their evening flight in praise of flight;
Then, strafing through the aerials and screaming
With full mouths, swifts drop in to catch them dreaming;
Below, a woman on a balcony reels
A trike down to a child – they watch its spinning wheels –
And I go visiting the inventive dead.
Two streets down, though, I think to dip my head
Like someone praying, in a basin, and
Yield to the perfumes of an alien hand,
And sacrifice some locks to elegance
Before the hypogean residence.
Its parlours are so quiet: the rich rooms,
Stripped of their furnishings, seem merely tombs.
The hosts are out – Are they at Naples too,
Leant on their tables, with their bones on view?
It's desolate without them: looking round
You're glad your terrace house is overground.
Seconds down here, and bowels start to churn,
Chests to strain: it's a struggle to return
Out of such iron hospitality
To the free air, and give the keeper back his key.

The luxury of getting lost! I check
Secretively the compass round my neck,
And find the Corso, and, half-dead, recover
Licking a cold white round thing like a lover,
Tenderly. An old man with much to say
Nods at the melting breast: "Inglese, Lei?"
And tells his travels. He left home to see
The blameless Ethiops; there his company
Enjoyed those beauties (black as black, tall, thin
And buttered) for a ravioli tin –

They don't like pasta, but they feast on what they get...
And he? I don't ask, but I sense regret
At missing – or at taking – his main chance
Of winning Africa and elegance.
He goes on through the desert and the sown,
The lands of memory that one seems to own:
Libya, Albania, Greece, and – if he'd gone –
The booming plains beyond the quiet Don,
But then was taken by his insolent friends
The Nazis, pointed to industrial ends
Among their slaves in factories and mines –
And just in time escaped between the lines
Of the Italian campaign. But why
Stay here? – since home's Palermo. "When I die"...
His eyes stray off. Beneath the status quo
Lie secrets that a stranger needn't know,
But moving, working still. I guess a state
Can clean it's own, but not a citizen's slate.
In the piazza, now, a screed's displayed
About the Independence Day parade:
The Fascist campaign-medals on one chest
Offended someone the régime oppressed.

The bright girls, dulled by evening, drain away –
The men, in economic mourning, stay –
I push through solemn circles down the street
But still must watch the news an hour, before we eat.
It seems so long a lesson, shown before
And shown again – What the Historian Saw:
The outvoted trying to impose a view
By tricks and violence, and (is this new?)
Others who care threatening not to care
(You can catch alienation anywhere).
We sit like children at the table, and wait;
The youngest player takes his pasta-plate
Out to the kitchen, sneaks some lettuce, cuts
It small, and forks it to his bellowing guts –
Which bellow louder, and he sneaks some more.
Is he a farmer's son? He's studying law
At Bari. After our bistecca, he
Recites the resonant names of Italy,
Right from Boethius. Paolo finds this idiotic,

But it's his trick and I'm Italian-patriotic,
Half-drunk on digestivo. The Signora's
Niece, a third-century beauty, sways before us,
Slim and tired from tennis; the girl who has
So achingly too much inside her bras
To play, brings back my shirts; and I arrange
My bill with cheques and fivers and small change.
I would get up so early – Did I kiss
The Signora goodnight? That memory's gone amiss.
Her conscript son, though, after his degree,
Invites himself to come and stay with me.

DAY XIII: Venerdì
(May 1, 1981)

Sometimes you curse all plans – but you obey
The self that planned, who couldn't know today
I would be here, not wanting to get up
From half a dream, and leave a tasted cup
To a bar sink (there's Paolo! – "Ciao!") and climb
Quick in a bus that comes ahead of time –
Six-ten! We rev and trumpet; through the glass
I spy a music, sun on lifted brass,
But can't hear if they celebrate hard labour,
The winner of our bread, or help a neighbour
To the necropolis, to dream his fill
Beyond the *Viaggio nell' Orgasmo* bill...

The old road shelves above – strata of dirt
Bulge out like petticoats from a fraying skirt;
I look up, shame-faced, till the road goes straight
For Andria (FIDELIS on its gate –
A food-shop selling Saracen take-aways –
A Rock-Shop – can't be offering what it says),
Then due north... Damn! what's this we're forking onto?
We're missing the cathedral of Bitonto!
And Ruvo! I'll come back, I'll bring my sposa,
As the Signora told me in Canosa.
But now I see, after three hundred miles,
Only the Adriatic, wreathed in smiles.

Barletta, Trani... The anxiety
Of getting nowhere starts to nibble me.
Someone suggests the Hotel History.
"Albergo della Storia?" "No! L'Astoria!"
Contented then, I nod through the emporia,
Bisceglie and Molfetta, ancient ports
Insensibly becoming new resorts.
Is this the peace that lasts a thousand years?
Barrage balloons (with fins, not cauliflower ears)
Point at a beach till everyone can spell
The patron saint of thirst: San Rafael;
Here, off the sand, under the pines, a poor
Family heaps needles in a cart (what for?);
There at our feet a round of football smoothes
A storm-creased river-bed, for fifty youths;
Curricles, trotting-horses; strand encumbered
With concrete calthrops, serially numbered;
The circonvallazione; and we come
To the new Christian town of Barium.

Relieved, the poet quits his glory-hole
At the Astoria, and resumes his role,
Scanning the sights. It's Friday: on the quay
They're selling jewels stolen from the sea:
Some lie uncut – raw rocks in pails; some, shiny
As sweets, and sold in packets they're so tiny,
Hang still unmelted in their water-purse;
Some look like English fish. The customers
Slip off with bags of prickly balls or stars
And lift them dripping over bows of cars.
Near me, a father bites an octopus
Leg off, handing his wife the sinuous
Body over his shoulder, as, mouth full, he pays.
The ill-dressed salesmen, proud of their displays,
Avoid our eyes, and turn their wealth, and stand
Aloof, as if they'd rather it were land.
Their lobsters make me long for delicate
Company. No one's caught a mermaid, but
The arches hid a flesh-pot, where they feed
The terrestrial man I am all he should need.

Women fill San Nicola's crypt. Incense

Reminds us the celestials go for scents,
The wise man's gift. I have to pray Saint Nicholas
Pardon: I can't take in his holy gas,
His blackened ladies and his gilded stones,
Just kneel and pay respect and see his bones,
And out.

By the Castello are the men
Of Bari, playing (Old v. New again)
A friendly, where the swifts join in: a high
Header's a pass to them and through the arc they fly.
The children watching, at least older ones,
With grandpas rouse the family champions,
Who jump, to strike a brief professional pose.
The youngest, round a pump, in party clothes,
Like bride and groom combining for the chores,
Play solemnly: she holds the tin, he pours.

For them, Mayday has brought the golden hour
Between necessities. I'm faltering now, a
Tremor of mind to warn the mind, before
It echoes in the lonely fuel-store:
Eat or break down. So I turn off to eat,
And find as well how old footballers use their feet:
To stand on. By his kiln, this gloomy fellow
Punches dough flat, pelts it with mozzarella
And golden-apple, and ("Is that you in
The cup-tie winners on the wall? – Turin?")
Furious with fortune, grunts he had a place.
(I take my reverent finger off his face.)

Back at the History, I find a queue
Of men who came here not to see but do,
With dark suits, solar calculators, plans
For the dénouement of the old romance:
They'll put the South out of its misery.

DAY XIV: Sabato
(May 2, 1981)

These are the hardest hours to justify,
Not envied by the dead – the hours I pass
Gaping at their possessions behind glass,
Windowshopping like Tantalus, an ape
That, hands in pockets, comprehends pure shape
Vacuously.
            A pretty secretary
Coasts by with papers rustling in a hurry
Daring a space-walk. From the airlock drifts
A fume of conversation. Off she lifts.

Two naked ladies wash a quacking bird
In a bowl. A satyr stands behind one, stirred:
His hands stretch to her buttocks.
                                        Helen hatches
From one egg, poised for international matches,
And from another the Dioscuri
Step, paired already, and paired perfectly.

A funeral helmet with its eyes too close – a
Warrior with strabismus? (from Canosa).
A penis moneybox (Egnazia). Suit
Of bronze (from Conversano) for minute
Head and unbending knees, nipples erect
For battle (fitted breastplate); would protect
The owner fully from all glancing blows.
And those containers, with great eyes, in rows,
Crowned with fresh dust, never again with wine,
Even for coins like these, if they were mine –
Struck for a city (dolphin) or a man
(Mark Antony, with ship; Octavian
On horseback; Lepidus – obscure) –
I'm hungry. I slide out to live some more.

Naturally, to live well you must repeat
Yourself – return to the good place to eat,
In this case. But the lovely stimuli
Just make the adventurous body sulk at me:
"I've had this." Then again I make it go

Not where it wants – some den – but to a show.
"Should be of interest, name not heard before –"
But: "Kaiser? An Expressionist? – equals Bore!
An exile too! Your century's full of them
And their deep-frozen tongues." My rule of thumb
Is to oppose the Id, and hope it's wrong,
But in the opera stalls *Fire* does seem long,
And empty as the house – with not a soul to meet.
Too bad next week I'm missing *Indiscreet*
Jewels (the Tuscan Regional Theatre, for a season):
Journey with Diderot on the Ways of Reason
And the Imaginary. Mangogul
And Mirzoza will keep the theatre full,
However full the dens are to discuss
This year's Translation of St Nicholas.

DAY XV: Domenica
(May 3, 1981)

How can Italians bear to say goodbye
So early Venus watches from the sky?
What a departure time! I stand and wait,
But no bus comes. Have I got up too late?
Oh God, it's Sunday! Everybody knows
Each week we imitate the gods' repose...
Not feeling very stoical, I begin
Yielding to Accidie (the traveller's sin)
And turning on my angel – when a coach
Rolls up behind, discreetly hissing a reproach.
Stammering, I ask the driver, does she go
To Brindisi? and in English he says: "No."
Spruce in his uniform, so Italian,
He tells me he's a Geordie (Bedlington!),
And married an Italian in the war.
Sounds like a story, so: "You fell on your
Feet there," I say; but he looks blank. I add,
"How nice to live here," and his face goes sad.
Well, after thirty-seven years, I guess
The words of nuptial envy don't impress:
Home isn't where he is, but where he wants to be.

Though I don't want to walk to Brindisi,
I grasp my bags, and savouring the pure
Air that absolves the grime of Via Cavour,
Set out: the station isn't far. Street-walls
Twinkle with printed trivia and thoughtful scrawls
In a late twentieth-century hand, the hand
That's cornered the epigraphy of the land.
There's lots to read here – and to sniff: débris
From last night's pleasure lies round bitterly.
Gradually, I'm convinced today's today.

But, on the platform, what's the paper say?
Everyone's got one; I must have one too,
And hear the sound-track I've been sleeping through.
Oh, a new book by Plutarch: the *Corriere*
Sees him as a provincial plagiary –
But, they like him...
                                        A flash among the trees:
Some ruin, passed with anaesthetic ease.
Under the trees, the soil's raked clear (a bed
For falling olives) or a sheet's been spread;
Few people out – they look up, short, robust,
In the dark colours fit for working dust,
Or, bright for Sunday, shade their motorbikes
And squirt the earth with what a handbook says it likes –
All with supporting kin at mass in shy
Small towns that barely swell against the sky –
Ceglie Messapico, San Vito dei
Normanni – lying low from history.

Brindisi! Even on the train I lose
All sense of ending: girls not wearing shoes,
The sort of girls you'd send to Outer Space
Pickled, to represent the human face –
Americans, tanned, a healthy negligence
Of their own beauty that inflames good sense –
Push past; the aisle jangles with instruments;
And other students clinging round the station
Depreciate it as a destination.
Embarked at, trampled through by migrant races,
It looks a place to leave, for other places.

Those girls stride off. Their bare feet make me so
Possessive! I stand aching as they go
With their young men... – To the worst hostelry
And the least generous beds in Brindisi...
– Perhaps they're pilgrims, with a vow... – That lass
Won't keep it if she steps on broken glass.

The Corso Garibaldi slumps straight down
From trains to ferries and bisects the town,
As planned in Rome – there's no one planning here.
The harbour's dead, and up some stairs the Via
Appia column terminally sways,
Sick of the bad air in these land-locked bays.
My heart sinks: no conclusion; just the flow
Of time over a world we cannot know;
The zero coated with imagination
Throws up a bitter taste of revelation.

Damn consequence (and lack of consequence)!
A man controls these hollow sentiments
With food: some fellow of another species
Will make me new – I'll eat some careless fishes.
I enter, scared, alone: the yellow cave's
Adorned with sea-things doomed to human graves.
Chilling – but soon my minestrone grin
Brings four Australians and three locals in.
The wine's good – and they top up my carafe.
I finish the Calvino book. I have
An honest-looking chordate grilled – a bream? –
When up the alley someone starts to scream.
Street-theatre? No: the three Apulians rise
And one goes to the door; we recognise
An older woman's wild vituperations,
A younger's sobs – a fight between relations;
Can't see a thing, he says – it's all indoors.
His friends tease him as if he were the cause.

A girl and three huge long-haired Goths take seats:
They just drink mineral water while she eats.
Seconds of mussels for the local men.
One waves for thirds.

The screams begin again.
But energy that excited us before
Has lost its reason. Now, it's first a bore,
Then worse, with breakage, terror, pleas for peace
Bellowed by neighbours. Sirens. The Police
(Squadra Volante) goggle, from their machines,
Like witnesses in going-to-heaven scenes.
Can't see the leading figures. Rude to stare.
I heard it. So I leave it in mid air.

Another woman's voice comes to my bed
And stops my fraternising with the dead
That afternoon. The listening-Tom deduces
(From tones across the air-well) mouth, lips, juices,
Amused and open spirit; splashes: he's
Growling out of the shower; she rolls at ease,
Flexed, strong, and laughing at the way he towers
Above her, rough, self-centred, for some hours.
– Or so I think, fleshing this arabesque
With Arab passports (seen at the front desk)...
Till, from my airwell window, I perceive
The water-noise was made by rain; the eave-
sdropped voices were the manager and his wife
In the kitchen, leading the Brindisian life.
I walk out, chastened.

Brindisi is full
Of foreigners (there ought to be a cull),
Whining for something, looking at the prices,
The faces and the forms and likely vices,
Or leaning on their vehicles in queues,
Considering travel-sickness, smokes and booze.
I sit in the piazza dedicated to
The first Italian king, Victor Emmanuel II,
Depressed. Distracted by the unholy sound
Of empty drink-tins being kicked around,
At first I don't take in who's kicking them:
Brindisi children.

And now night has come,
The Corso's effortlessly taken back
In triumph from the rangy alien pack

By Sunday crowds. Families, ages, classes
Are trading smiles and handshakes, ices, glasses.
In the whole street one boy's exchanging chaff
With travelling girls. His friends, embarrassed, laugh.
Trails of home-cooking thread the atmosphere,
And tame the place.

For some, the end is here.

Notes

This poem is as unobscure and impersonal as I could make it, but what I think is general knowledge may well not be general knowledge. I have tried therefore to guess where pleasure would be released by a soupçon of information, and provided a note.

At some points in the poem I have cannibalised or otherwise reworked phrases from the Horace poem which gave me my route (*Satires* I, 5). I have drawn attention to some of these parallels, mostly in the form "Horace" with a line-number.

Readers interested in Horace's predecessor Lucilius can find what is left of his work in the Loeb Classical Library *Remains of Old Latin*, edited and translated by E.H. Warmington, Vol.III, 1938.

For more information on places in the poem I can recommend William Smith's admirable *Dictionary of Greek and Roman Geography*, 2 vols., 1854-7, which somebody ought to reprint. There is no modern book on the Via Appia; in fact, there has only ever been one (Pratilli, 1745), which I did not use. After ploughing through a bog of learned articles and many travel-books of various dates, all covering only sections of my route, I can say that by far the most useful book to me (apart from Smith's *Dictionary*) was Baedeker's 1896 guide to South Italy. Some other debts are mentioned in their places in these Notes.

All errors are my own.

p.111 "Flying from great Newcastle...bed" These lines imitate the beginning of Horace's poem. They were written after I had phoned Ariccia from Newcastle to book a room.

"familiar Latin" The idea of birds singing "their Latin" (their song) is common in mediaeval French and troubadour poetry. I thought I had seen it in English too, but seem to have been mistaken.

"Bellow" "Bello" is the Italian for handsome or beautiful. I was trying to provide myself with a companion like Horace's Heliodorus, "most learned of the Greeks" (Horace, 3).

p.112 "lake, dull as old mercury" The Lago di Nemi has been

called the Mirror of Diana for at least sixteen centuries (since Servius). Diana had a famous temple there with a high-priest who was a runaway slave (see J.G. Frazer, *The Golden Bough*).

"beggar" This slope (clivus Aricinus) was a haunt of beggars in classical times because rich people's carriages could only go slowly up the steep road.

"Ariccia church... steps" These steps were a favourite seat for Ibsen in the first intervals of *Brand*, that is, while he was writing it. Presumably the delightful pavilion-like rooms at each end of the façade were not then used as bars, but that small piazza, now ruined by traffic, would have been the centre of Ariccian life when Ibsen lived there (1865).

"Menotti Garibaldi" Garibaldi's son was honoured by a statue there rather than in Velletri (which he represented as Deputato for many years) because he had a farm at Albano and lived there.

p.113 "Legs as long as mine... ease... barge across these marshes" These phrases all refer to remarks in Horace.

The last line of Day II is related to one of Auden's in "Letter to Lord Byron", Part IV (Auden and MacNeice, *Letters from Iceland*, 1937, p.205).

"Valley of the Latin Muse" The Via della Valle delle Camene runs southwards by the Via della Terme di Caracalla (which covers the old Via Appia at this point). For this day's walk see Georgina Masson's *The Companion Guide to Rome*, 6th ed. 1980.

p.114 "Hic soror et frater" "Here (lie buried) a sister and a brother..."

"Coraggio! Su!... Thank God!" Cf. *Acts of the Apostles* Chapter 28, 15: "And from thence, when the brethren heard of us, they came to meet us as far as Appii Forum, and The three taverns: whom when Paul saw, he thanked God, and took courage." The conversation I report took place within ten miles of Rome. Appii Forum (Horace, 3) is forty-three Roman miles down the Appian Way, and the Tres Tabernae are thirty-three miles (i.e., both are beyond Ariccia).

"marking time" At this stage in the journey I thought I should try whenever possible to synchronise exactly with Horace, arriving for instance at Terracina on the fourth evening as he did.

"Benito's" By the way, I can thoroughly recommend Benito's restaurant (in Velletri) and his hotel "in the wood" (up a side road to the left as you come into Velletri from the north).

p.115 "magic mountain" This is Monte Circeo now a national park, but supposedly the place where Circe turned some of Odysseus's companions into pigs (*Odyssey* X; *Aeneid* VII, 10-20).

"Merlino" My use of this graffito is, I am afraid, frivolous – I never found out what Merlin was accused of.

"CXX" The Terracina promontory was cut back from the shoreline by Trajan's engineers so that travellers would no longer have the trouble (as Horace did) of climbing up and over this last ridge of the Volscian mountains. The engineers carved the rock-face with a series of graduated numerals, the purpose of which is still uncertain.

"Napoli merda" "The Naples team stinks."

"Montale's prose" For example his charming sketches translated as *The Butterfly of Dinard*(London Magazine editions, 1970).

p.116 "trucidati dai tedeschi" "slaughtered by the Germans."

"ancient red" In museums, ancient inscriptions in worn stone are often made more legible by the use of red paint of some kind; apparently this repeats ancient practice.

"what kind of palms" I was thinking of Goethe's interest, when he first came to Italy in 1786, in finding the "primeval plant" from which all other plants might be derived. (Palms belong to one of the oldest plant groups.)

"S.P.Q.T." Senatus Populusque Tarracinensis, the senate and the people of what we now call Terracina. (The Volsci called it Anxur.) The formula SPQR is still used by the municipality of Rome (e.g., on manholes).

p.117 "beardless" I was intrigued by Juppiter Imberbis, the dedicatee of the temple, because after fifteen years of wearing a beard I had recently become clean-shaven, partly because of this journey.

"reptiles...a man creeps" References to creeping or crawling, in this part of the poem, are Horatian (line 25).

p.118 "the damn-fool writer" See Horace (35).

p.119 "the broken castle" This is where the first Anti-pope was elected in 1378, causing the great Schism. Also it was the home of the beautiful countess Giulia Gonzaga (wife of Vespasiano Colonna), whose fame attracted the attention of the Saracen corsair Haireddin Barbarossa in 1534. He thought she would make a nice present to the Sultan of Constantinople; but she escaped, and he burnt Fondi in disgust.

"collirio" Horace (30) rubbed the same stuff in his eyes in 37 BC here.

"Hog-calls" is a reminder of the men Circe turned into boars.

p.120 "dangerous inns of Terracina" Cf. Auber's opera *Fra Diavolo*, based on a Washington Irving story ("The Inn of Terracina").

Sperlonga is ancient Spelunca, where Tiberius had a villa "which derived its name from a natural cave or grotto in which the emperor used to dine and where he on one occasion very nearly lost his life, by the falling in of the roof of the cavern" (Smith's *Dictionary*, under Spelunca). The well-known statue of Laocoon and his sons being constricted by a seasnake was found here.

p.121 "Gaeta" – named after Aeneas' nurse, Caieta, who was buried here (*Aeneid* VII,2), hence the appropriateness of seeing a breast (and a Gulf, since the word comes from the Greek for bosom). The Sirens lived further south – *Aeneid* V, 864 – between Sorrento and Capri.

"cicerone" Cicero had a villa at Formiae, a fashionable resort at the time, and was murdered on the roadside somewhere near, a victim of the proscriptions of the Triumvirs in 43 BC. (No Horatian comment.)

"goddesses" The nymph Marica, mother of King Latinus (Aeneas' father-in-law), used to bathe in the Garigliano (then called the Liris). The river was one of the most bitterly contested boundaries in Italy during the Second World War, and there are large military cemeteries just downstream from ancient Minturnae (the theatre mentioned). "The Garigliano cure" is the sort of joke I imagine the soldiers made to each other as they fought through the mud in January and February 1944. The buffaloes, by the way, produce the milk from which mozzarella is made.

p.122 "coincidence" "Coincidenza" is the Italian for "connection" in the sense of train time-tables. It was from this point that in spite of anxiety I realised I could trust "fate" or my "travel angel" to give me material for my poem, if not a good time.

"taste the salt of" *"come sa di sale/lo pane altrui, e com' è duro calle/lo scendere e il salir per l'altrui scale'* (Dante, *Paradiso*, XVII, 58-).

"Orazio met Virgilio" on the coast at Sinuessa, near Mondragone (Horace, 40).

p.123 "Capua" This is a confusing place-name: the old city of Capua was destroyed by the Saracens in 841, and the surviving inhabitants moved a few miles to Casilinum and changed its name to Capua. So modern Capua is ancient Casilinum. Then ancient Capua revived and is now called Santa Maria Capua Vetere. There are excellent stories about both places in Livy's account of the Second Punic War (e.g. in Book XXIII).

"Capua Gate" means Frederic II's triumphal gateway on the north bank of the Volturno at Capua (Casilinum).

"luxury hotel" Hannibal was said to have been defeated not by Roman valour but by luxuria Campana (Livy XXIII, xlv), the dolce vita of Capua, where his men spent a winter whose pleasures they couldn't get over.

"earthquake day" Sunday November 23, 1980. The epicentre was about fifty miles further south, in the Apennines.

"Hotel Capys" named after the legendary founder of Capua.

"letto matrimoniale" i.e., at last the double-bed promised for Day I.

The "narrow railway line" I found was, I think, the one used by Garibaldi to transport troops around the battle-field at the Battle of the Volturno, October 1 1860. (See G.M. Trevelyan's *Garibaldi and the making of Italy*, 1911.)

p.124 "slave . . . sword . . . chains" This is my unHoratian way of not-mentioning the gladiatorial schools of Capua or the slaves' revolt (under Spartacus) which began here a few years before Virgil was born.

"something vague au naturel" Garibaldi was given a "vague" meal of figs and a glass of water in the high street near the piazza del 1 Ottobre 1860 (where the agricultural machinery was on show) by an Englishwoman called Jessie White. She held it up to him as he sat on his horse, surrounded by the local band which continued to play all day in spite of being under fire.

The "Restaurant Faust" was recommended by my guide-book (Peter Gunn, *The Companion Guide to Southern Italy*, 1969) – a book I found unhelpful on the journey.

p.125 "orange skin" I think these Asians must have been "boat-people", refugees from North Vietnam.

"one sad man" Democritus was, I think, the first person to claim he found the audience more interesting than the play. (See Horace *Epistles* II, 1, 197.) On the other hand, he was not the "crying philosopher" but the laughing one.

p.127 "medicina estetica" "Aesthetic medicine" is what "beauticians" sell, in Italy.

"to see the stars again" Cf. last line of Dante's *Inferno*.

"The radio bird" is a station call-sign; I think it is broadcast just before the news or to mark programme changes.

p.128 "Olympus" My camera.

"sunken roads" These are a feature of the soft volcanic plain. They have been there since at least the third century BC.

p.130 "Dolphins" This is the design on one of the lowest-denomination Italian coins (five lire?).

"a wrecked building... concrete graves" These landmarks (mentioned again in a few pages) seemed to me to be possibly one of the Garibaldian artillery positions described by G.M. Trevelyan in his account of the Battle of the Volturno.

"other older men" I was rather conscious that Hannibal, Garibaldi and Trevelyan had preceded me up this hill, and wondered how old they had been at the time.

p.131 "amphitheatre" This is the building I could only see the outside of at Santa Maria Capua Vetere (Capua).

p.133 "erba medica" I was excited that after two millennia there was still a kind of "grass" ("medick" in English) with the same name it has in Virgil (*Georgics* 1, 215), even if those who fed it to their animals did not know it came from Media (Persia, Iran) originally.

p.135 "Ma che biglietto?..." "Ticket be damned. Don't travel today. Bad luck." The word cattivo (bad, or naughty) derives from captivus.

"Non son buona" "I'm not good"

"Misreading splashes like a Saracen" Was the water going from left to right or right to left (like Islamic script)?

p.136 "broken bridge" Mentioned because possibly one of the ruined Roman bridges on Horace's road.

p.137 "Calvino's story" One of the stories in *Cosmicomiche*, a wonderful book of reminiscences about the early history of the universe.

"To have a stone thrown at you" Like Manfred, whose soldiers covered his corpse with a huge cairn of stones from the river-bed after his defeat at Benevento. (See Dante, *Purgatorio*, III, 127-9.) The stone thrown at me reminded me strongly of bad times in Iran.

"an ill wind" Benevento's name doesn't mean anything to do with good winds or welcome. It is a euphemistic change imposed by the Romans on the previous name, Malventum or Maleventum, which sounded unlucky to a Latin speaker. Maleventum is in turn a Latinisation of what may be the foundation-name of the town, Maloenton, apparently Greek and meaning possibly "the return of the flocks".

p.138 "an old friend" I was thinking of Odysseus' Trojan-war comrade Diomedes, who is credited with founding Benevento as well as other south Italian cities. Odysseus' embarrassed nakedness when meeting Nausicaa and her hand-maidens is related in *Odyssey* VI.

"Santa Sofia" I hope my homage to Sofia Loren ("la bella pizzaiola puteolana" as Marino Marini called her in a lovely song) doesn't obscure my homage to the eighth-century church of the Holy Wisdom, one of the most beautiful buildings I have seen. Puteoli (Miss Loren's Pozzuoli) is where Virgil lived at the time of Horace's journey; it is just north of Naples.

"the Trajana" A restaurant near Trajan's triumphal arch, which is one of the sights of Benevento and is the ancient exit from town of the Appian Way.

"escape by bus" A further hint of paranoia here. In fact the lack of buses going east from Benevento to the Adriatic is presumably caused by the excellence of the train service, and its directness.

"Sirenland" I mean the Neapolitan area (cf. Norman Douglas, *Siren Land*, 1911).

p.139 "Holy Ghost" The Santo Spirito branch-banks in Terracina and in Benevento rejected my traveller's cheques.

p.140 "not a name to say to ladies" This is the first of a number of hints at the name of the town where I spent that night. The idea of not naming it comes from Horace (87), who got it from Lucilius, who got it from Archestratus. Many towns have been suggested as the one he stayed at: I just chose the most interesting one of these.

"Greci" There were Albanians here when the philosopher Berkeley passed this way in May 1717. (The travel-journal is in Vol. VII of his *Works*, edited by A.A. Luce, 1955.)

"Benevento leaves" This is where Horace's route branches left from the Via Appia proper (which continues south to Taranto before turning across the heel to Brindisi). The exact line of Horace's route is still obscure – to say the least.

p.141 "Homewards" Horace was born at Venusia (Venosa), not far from here; as he says, "Apulia begins to show me the mountains I know" (line 77).

"the Chess Pitch" "Il Tavoliere", so called because of its regular ancient layout of roads, allotments and canals – centuriation, still very clear from above.

"invisible town" a reference to another Calvino book.

"the local wind" Horace calls it Atabulus (78).

p.143 "Furbo" "clever", disapproving and admiring at the same time.

"noble sole" This is my tribute to Lucilius (Book III, fragment 124), who mentions the "honestas plantas" of a lady innkeeper in his travel poem.

p.145 "Herdonia" This ancient place-name is another of those suggested for the place Horace stayed at but couldn't name in verse.

"Islamic bridge" Roman, of course, like the triumphal arch a few lines further on.

p.146 "rich menus" John of Salisbury mentions an amazing meal he had here with ingredients coming from "Constantinople, Babylon, Alexandria, Palestine, Tripolitania, Syria, Phenicia – as if Sicily, Calabria, Apulia and Campania couldn't produce the makings of a delicate meal" (*Policraticus*, III, vii, 735d). He was in the company of the treasurer of York Cathedral.

p.147 "the dialogue" The coach's rather pushy manner of arguing reminded me of Plato's characterisation of Socrates in the *Republic*.

"Lucanian cows" This is what the Romans called elephants when they first saw them in Pyrrhus' army – and it is what these cathedral elephants looked like. (Cf. Lucretius, V, 1302.)

p.149 "take the gift of sleep" This Homeric phrase I found in the *Iliad* (last line of Book VII for instance) when checking up on Diomedes' exploits against Aphrodite and Ares.

"breakfast is best . . . " This, including the simile about the sun, is adapted from the start of Pindar's first *Olympic Ode* ("Water is best . . . "). The Day is as Greek as I could decently make it, given that Diomedes founded this city (Horace, 92).

"Hector Proudfly Street" Via Ettore Fieramosca sounds very Scottish in translation. Fieramosca was the leader of thirteen Italian champions who beat a boastful team of French knights near Barletta in 1503. The chevalier sans peur et sans reproche, Bayard, was one of the umpires at this contest.

"our founder . . . the worst goddess . . . the worst god" *Iliad* V is about Diomedes' bravery against these gods, and various Trojans.

"balances" An image from Aeschylus (*Agamemnon* 439).

p.150 "Swabian... Norman" Swabian refers to Frederick II (Stupor Mundi) and Norman refers to Bohemond (son of Robert Guiscard): I think both had fortifications of some sort here.

"lingua" Italian dialect-speakers call the national version of the language "lingua", as if it were human speech par excellence. I mention this because Horace (*Satires* I, 10,30) calls the Canosans bilingual.

p.151 "to see the blameless Ethiops" In both of Homer's poems gods go from Olympus to visit the Ethiops for a good feast.

p.153 "FIDELIS" Faithful to Frederick II, that is.

"Bitonto" Martial (II, 48) was pretty rude about Butunti, but since his time it has acquired a very fine Romanesque cathedral.

"Ruvo" After a night at Canosa, Horace and his friends spent the next night (line 94) at Rubi (another Romanesque cathedral).

p.154 "circonvallazione" The word means "ring-road", but it chimes well with Horace's mention (97) of the "fortifications" (*moenia*) of "fishy Bari".

"new Christian town" By this I mean that the bus dropped us all off in the new town. The old town is not just pre-Christian; it is pre-Greek.

p.155 "solar calculators" Pocket calculators that run on solar batteries.

p.157 "the Translation" The annual festival of the *Transfer* of St Nicholas' bones from Myra to Bari. St. Nicholas is of special interest to a Newcastle person because he is the dedicatee of our cathedral.

"stoical" cf. Horace, lines 101-3.

p.159 "careless fishes" cf. *Iliad* XXI, 123, where the adjective means not "careless" but "care-free and without relatives".

p.161 "For some, the end" Including Virgil, who died in Brindisi on September 21, 19 BC. (see Hermann Broch's novel, *The Death of Virgil*, translated by J.S. Untermeyer, 1946).

"the end is here" This bears some relation to Horace's last line: *Brundisium longae finis chartaeque viaeque est*, "Brindisi is the end of both my long screed and my journey".

Acknowledgements

I am grateful to the editors or literary editors of the journals in which many of these poems first appeared, and to the publishers of the three books reprinted or excerpted from, Ceolfrith Press (*Contentions*) and Secker and Warburg (*Talking Back* and *On the Appian Way*). The poem "Talking to Bede" is still in print separately as a pamphlet with notes (Ashington, MidNAG).

Of the uncollected poems, "At Sea" has appeared as a broadside, published by Occasional Works, and also in the Poetry Book Society Supplement, Christmas 1986. Others have appeared or been accepted to appear in *the Times Literary Supplement, New Statesman, PN Review, London Magazine, The Observer, Poetry Durham, Harvard Magazine, Spectator, Margin, Poetry Review, Encounter,* and *London Review of Books*. A number were broadcast by the BBC Radio 3 programme *Poetry Now*.

I am most grateful to the Ingram Merrill Foundation for a generous grant which enabled me to collect material for "a book of unified poems about America" (meaning the United States) in 1983 and 1984; and to the Djerassi Foundation for delightful hospitality in California in the spring of 1984. Section I of this book contains the poems of that "unified book" that have been written so far.

Perhaps here I should also express again my gratitude to the Arts Council of Great Britain for an award in 1979 and to Northern Arts for help with my travelling expenses in Italy in 1981.

